THE FIRST AND BEST BUDDHIST TEACHINGS

From the oldest sacred book in Buddhist Literature—
The Sutta Nipata, great psychological and spiritual insights
address some of the deepest concerns of our time and
offer practical solutions to the problems that
plague our world today.

THE FIRST AND BEST

BUDDHIST TEACHINGS

Sutta Nipata Selections and Inspired Essays

SUSUNAGA WEERAPERUMA

New Age Books

ISBN: 81-7822-257-4

First Edition: Delhi, 2006

Cover Design By Claudia Weeraperuma

Published by
NEW AGE BOOKS
A-44 Naraina Phase I
New Delhi-110 028 (INDIA)
Email: nab@vsnl.in
Website: www.newagebooksindia.com

Printed in India
at Shri Jainendra Press
A-45 Naraina Phase-I, New Delhi-110 028

Contents

PART II
THE SUTTA NIPATA: SOME SELECTIONS

Acknowledgements

My grateful thanks to my wife Dr Claudia Weeraperuma, who painstakingly revised and edited the manuscript, added a few symbolic illustrations of hers, and later transferred the entire text onto the computer. She also spent many hours helping me to trace very valuable sources of information during the course of the last few years.

Preface

More than half of this book consists of selections from the *Sutta Nipata* and my commentaries thereon. Extraordinarily profound is the *Sutta Nipata*, which is the oldest sacred tome in Buddhist literature. It is a particularly authentic version of the Buddha's discourses, because of its antiquity, language, style and contents. In my commentaries I have tried to express the ancient wisdom in the idiom of our time. One has to go *beyond* the words of these very powerful verses and understand their hidden meanings intuitively.

There is a popular misconception that Buddhism is a rather airy-fairy intellectual system that is out of touch with the harsh realities of life. This impression is totally untrue. I have tried to demonstrate that the Buddha was a very practical person in the chapter *Facing Death: Kisagotami's Problem.* He handled her psychological crisis by asking her to do something. She had to carry out a task. Kisagotami had been inconsolable when her beloved son died. Refusing to accept the inevitability of death, she had the fanciful notion that the boy was only ill and would soon return to normacy. Carrying the corpse in her arms, she had approached the Buddha, who had realised that the poor woman was still too distraught to think clearly about her dear son's demise. The Buddha did *not* preach her a sermon, as would have been his usual practice, but instructed her to get some mustard seeds from a house wherein none had ever died. She went in search of such a house but without success. Realising the sheer impossibility of finding a household that had never been touched by death, Kisagotami eventually understood the fact of impermanence—the great truth of *Anicca* concerning the rising, changing and passing of things. Existence is never permanent. All existence is impermanent. All formations are transitory. As Nirvana is neither a formation nor a conditioned state, Nirvana alone is permanent.

Of the numerous definitions of religion that are in existence, my favourite definition is quite a simple one. Real religion is nothing but *how* you conduct yourself in everyday life. A truly religious person, in other words, leads a life that is infused with a moral sense. What matters is not the belief in this, that and the other, but whether or not we are really righteous and feel compassion for all living beings. This profound truth was well expressed by the Master:

> *Better than leading an immoral life lasting for one hundred years,*
> *is one single day devoted to virtue and meditation.*
>
> –Dhammapada, 110

Purity in thought, word and deed is one of the central themes in the *Sutta Nipata.* Morality or virtue is a *sine qua non* of Nirvana. Purity is not the outcome of the brutal repression of all that is negative or unwholesome in the psyche, but the intelligent and insightful recognition of their existence, or the awareness of one's negative traits fully, and the consequent elimination of them. The perfume of purity is born of understanding.

Watchful intelligence is meditation. Are we always watchful and alert? Are we always awake? By being alert and by spotting what is bad within us, the mind automatically gets cleansed of its troublesome traits.

Such is the degeneracy of our times that the vast majority in both the East and the West are obsessed with money-making. The modern ethic, alas, seems to be to amass wealth as hurriedly as possible by hook or by crook. Our relentless pursuit of power, position, profit and pleasure verges on the neurotic. Gone are the times when what we valued most in life was the true, the good and the beautiful. In the *Sigalovada Sutta,* which has been the inspiration for the chapter *Recipe for a Happy Society,* the

Buddha examined social interactions from a highly ethical standpoint.

The entire *Sigalovada Sutta* is about the correct or the *right* way of worshipping the directions. In this essay I have used the word "worship" not literally but figuratively. Instead of reverentially bowing before the various directions, the Buddha told Sigalaka that worshipping consists in leading a *righteous* life —there are many moral things that must be done and a great number of immoral things that should be avoided. The Buddha clearly demonstrated the absolute meaninglessness of practising the ancient Vedic ritual of worshipping the different directions. Yet, because the Buddha fully understood the tradition-bound mindset of Sigalaka, the Teacher used the *form* of the ritual when delivering this discourse. But the deeper meaning as well as the substance of the rituals, as explained by the Buddha, was very new and completely different from how it had been understood for centuries.

In the sphere of ethics, an attitude of reverence for all forms of life is a matter of supreme importance. Caring Buddhists never do anyone any harm in thought, word or deed. The word 'anyone' is all-inclusive in the sense that it not only includes human beings but also non-humans, such as animals, insects, birds, reptiles, fish and the like. Their all-embracing compassion transcends all man-made barriers based on caste, class, creed, race or nationality.

> *All fear danger. All love life. Therefore neither kill nor cause to kill.*
>
> –Dhammapada, 130

The karmic consequences of killing have been described in the chapter *The Buddha Denounced the Destruction of Life.*

Genuine Buddhists, needless to say, are strict vegetarians. They naturally avoid like the plague the taking of foods that have directly or indirectly involved the killing of animals. Their vegetarianism springs from their compassionate nature. Besides, they cannot bear the thought that the nicely spiced or tastily flavoured dead animals that have ended up on their plates might well have been their close friends or relations in previous lives.

Kind-hearted Buddhists would also strongly disapprove of the production and sale of armaments. In addition, even if being a pacifist becomes a punishable offence, they would always refuse to support war with all its concomitant violence, loss of lives and miseries. In connection with these problems, I wish to refer the reader to two chapters—*In Praise of Pacifism* and *Buddhist Blueprint for World Peace.*

In this book I have reproduced the full texts of letters that I wrote in response to two urgent inquiries. The chapter *Why Worry about Growing Old?* was my long reply to a lady of Austrian origin. Her advancing years unduly troubled her. In the course of my reply, among other things, I stated that "the constant renewal of the mind is as important as the constant regeneration of the body. For instance, if we fail to let go the dead past, if we do not throw away the long accumulated cravings and bitter resentments, not excluding our minor resentments, then all these, like deeply disturbed ghosts, will always haunt and trouble the psyche not only in the remaining years of this life but also in the lives to come."

A chronic depressive from distant Iceland wrote to me that she was desperately unhappy. In the chapter *Why Suffer from Depression?* I adopted a Buddhist approach to her problem. The suggested solution was mindfulness or meditation, which is sometimes better described as awareness. This question is discussed again in the chapter *Modus Operandi of Meditation.*

Meditation is the key to Nirvana.

— SUSUNAGA WEERAPERUMA

Part I

INSPIRED ESSAYS

1

Ananda : Rememberer of the Dharma

Ananda was one of the greatest disciples of the Buddha. Ananda and the Buddha had a lot in common. They came to earth from the Tusita heaven; they were born on the same day; they belonged to the warrior caste of the Sakyan royal family. They were first cousins because Ananda's father Amitodana was the brother of Suddhodana – the Buddha's father.

In the belief that the boy would be a bringer of joy and happiness, he was named Ananda, which also means bliss of ecstasy.

Soon after his ordination, Ananda became a 'stream-winner', attaining the first stage of sainthood after listening to a discourse of the Elder Punna.

Ananda was thirty-seven when he joined the order of monks. Ananda started purifying his mind immediately after becoming a monk. He was such a good teacher of the Dharma that the Buddha would sometimes ask Ananda to act on his behalf. As the Master was not feeling well on one occasion he said, "Ananda, talk about the disciple in higher training. I have to stretch myself as I am suffering from back pain." At the end of Ananda's talk, the Buddha exclaimed, "Excellent, Ananda, excellent!"

Unfortunately the Buddha did not have a regular attendant for the first twenty years following his Illumination. Different monks had attended the Buddha at various times. Some of them were unsatisfactory. However, at the age of fifty-five, when he was in advanced years, the Buddha gave Ananda the task of being his permanent attendant. It must be said that Ananda did his duties excellently. Ananda was not so much acting out of duty as expressing his unbounded affection for the Buddha.

Ananda realised that there might be some murmurs of discontent if he became the Teacher's personal attendant. In order to dissuade people from remarking, "who would not like to be the Buddha's personal attendant, if thereby one can enjoy certain advantages and privileges?" Ananda offered his services to the Buddha with the following 8 stipulations:

1. The Buddha must not give Ananda robes that the former had received.
2. The Buddha must not give him food that the former had received.
3. The Buddha must not permit Ananda to share a room with him.
4. Ananda must not accompany the Buddha whenever the latter is invited.
5. When Ananda is invited, the Buddha must accompany him.
6. The Buddha must allow Ananda to introduce visitors from afar who wished to meet the Buddha.
7. The Buddha must permit Ananda to meet him whenever doubts arise.
8. The Buddha must repeat to Ananda the discourses that had been delivered in his absence.

The Buddha agreed to all the foregoing conditions. Ananda served him with undeviating devotion. Ananda always felt a great loyalty to the Buddha. On account of their close association it was Ananda who knew the Teacher best. He had the great privilege of being the Buddha's personal attendant for 25 years.

The Buddha selected Ananda as his personal attendant because he was the most suitable person for this purpose. It was not a nepotistic choice on the Buddha's part. Ananda waited on the Buddha out of loving concern for the Master. Ananda would bring him water for washing his face, and provide him with toothpicks for cleaning his teeth. He would not only clean his cell but also wash his feet. It was also necessary to fan him when it was too hot. Sometimes the Buddha's back would ache and Ananda would massage him; he would obtain medicines when the Buddha was ill.

The Buddha remarked that Ananda was foremost among his disciples in six respects — erudition, the ability to remember, good behaviour and quick wit, resoluteness and caring.

The following incident illustrates his wit. Ananda requested water from Pakati, a girl of 'low' caste. The embarrassed girl said, "O nobleman, as I belong to the Matanga caste, I am too humble and mean to serve you water." Ananda quipped, "Sister, what I requested was not caste but water!"

A good-looking monk with a certain charm, Ananda was liked a lot by many. He was a real asset to the Sangha. An able preacher with a beautiful voice, many women — including queens, princesses and nuns — were attracted to him. Ananda remained calm. He was unaffected by their burning passion for him. They failed to tempt him away from the path of purity.

Ananda declared:

> *"I was a learner for twenty-five years;*
> *No carnal desires disturbed me."*
>
> — Psalms of the Brethren, 1039

While preaching a sermon to a certain nun, Ananda remarked that Arhatship definitely cannot be attained by means of sex:

> *"Sister, this body came into existence*
> *Because of the sexual act,*
> *But the Buddha has said*
> *That the bridge should be destroyed."*
>
> — Anguttara Nikaya IV, 159

Tantric sexual union, needless to say, has no place whatsoever in Buddhism. On the contrary, one has to transcend all forms of craving (*Tanha*) in order to reach the other shore. So clever, subtle and resourceful is the mind that it can invent a thousand reasons and numerous excuses for giving expression to sexual desires, all nicely disguised as 'spiritual practices'!

> *"What is the origin of suffering?*
> *It is craving,*
> *Which results in rebirth,*
> *And involved with pleasure and lust,*

Finding fresh pleasure now in this, now in that:
In other words, sensual craving,
Craving for existence, and craving for non-existence."
— Digha Nikaya 22

During the last days of the Buddha, Ananda posed the following interesting and important question: "Lord, how should we behave towards women?"

"Don't see them, Ananda."
"Lord, in case we see them, how should we behave?"
"Don't talk with them, Ananda."
"Lord, in case they talk with us, how should we behave?"
"Be mindful, Ananda."
— Mahaparinibbana Sutta 5.9

The above-mentioned advice is presumably applicable to each and every situation in life, including those in which a man speaks with a woman.

Mindfulness at all times and in all circumstances is a *sine qua non* for leading the meditative and holy life. Just being watchful of oneself, seeing how thoughts, feelings and sensations arise and fall, which is called self-observation, is the essence of meditation. When there is full awareness of the thought-process, or, the simple observation of the thought-process, the mere watching of it, neither indulgently nor censoriously, but by just allowing the stream to operate fully and freely, then the very movement of this restless river tends to slow down. Consequently, the whole process, of its own accord, grinds to a halt.

Ananda made possible the establishment of the order of nuns. A number of women led by Mahapajapati Gotami, the Buddha's step-mother, approached the Buddha and requested permission to begin such an order. Thrice Mahapajapati Gotami appealed to the Buddha and thrice he turned her down.

Mahapajapati Gotami and her entourage were standing outside the monastery where the Buddha was in residence. Her feet were swollen. The lady was crying. Ananda inquired about the cause of her disturbed state. She said that the Master had rejected her plea for an order of nuns. Deeply moved by her story, Ananda decided to intercede with the Buddha on her behalf.

Thrice Ananda repeated her request but each time the Buddha answered in the negative. Thereupon Ananda argued, "if a woman were to renounce the world and enter the state of homelessness in the teachings and the discipline of the Buddha, is she capable of becoming a stream-enterer, a once-returner, a non-returner or an Arhat?" When the Buddha said that that was true, Ananda proceeded to speak pleadingly, "if a woman were capable of such attainments, it would be good if you would allow women to lead the homeless lives of nuns. Besides, Mahapajapati Gotami has served you well — she was your aunt, governess and nurse who fed you with her own milk after your mother's passing away." The Buddha agreed reluctantly, stating that because of the decision to have an order of nuns, the system or dispensation would last only five hundred years instead of a thousand. The Buddha also stipulated eight conditions so that only the best women would agree to them. There was also going to be a strict separation of the sexes in the Sangha.

Long before the advent of feminism in the world, Ananda had been a champion of women's rights — not the mere mundane right to have equal pay for equal work and the like that are designed to improve the political, social and economic status of women, invaluable though these rights are, but much more importantly, to give women the chance to transcend material concerns and face the other shore.

Soon after the passing away of the Buddha the First Council was held at Rajagaha to preserve the purity of the teachings. Mahakassapa presided over the assembled monks and we know that Ananda played an important role in it.

Although Mahakassapa was not present at Kusinagara where the Buddha had breathed his last, he was proceeding to that place with a large retinue. When a naked ascetic conveyed the sad news that the Buddha was no more, some of the monks started lamenting loudly. But the monk Subhadda asked them to stop this needless expression of grief. He remarked that they would now be free to do exactly as they pleased, especially because the deceased Master used to criticise their unworthy behaviour. They would no longer be treated as schoolboys who had gone astray. These words of Subhadda alarmed Mahakassapa, who started concerning himself with the problem of ensuring the purity and authenticity of the Buddha's teachings for the benefit of posterity.

Only Arhats were eligible to participate in the First Council's proceedings, and 499 Arhats were already present. Doubting his suitability to participate in the discussions of the Council, Ananda stayed up late and immersed himself in meditation. He was painfully aware that he was not yet an Elder or Arhat. Enthusiastically he worked very hard. While staying on a terrace he continued delving into himself far into the night. His efforts were still without fruition. He entered the Vihara and sat on his couch. He moved his body and he wished to lie down. There was a moment when his head had not yet reached the pillow, nor were his feet raised from the floor. Exactly then all his samsaric stains left his mind and heart. Thus purified, Ananda attained Illumination. Thereafter he went into the hall of the First Council.

It is necessary to reiterate that the monks who gathered at Rajagaha were all Arhats. It was only after attaining Arhatship that Ananda was deemed ready to appear before the Council for the purpose of answering questions. Therefore most of the discourses in the Buddhist scriptures begin with Ananda's famous opening line "Thus have I heard" (*evam me sutam*).

At the First Council Ananda was questioned and his answers settled the substance of the *Sutta Pitaka*, which is a collection of all the Buddha's discourses (including talks by some of his outstanding disciples such as Sariputta and Mogallana). Ananda also answered questions relating to the occasion of the discourses and the person or persons to whom they were delivered.

We are deeply indebted to Ananda for our knowledge of what the Buddha actually said. Thanks to his extraordinarily prodigious memory, he was able to recall the entirety of each discourse from memory. When Mahakassapa questioned Ananda, the latter was able to recite accurately the Master's sermons and conversations.

When he was asked how many of the Master's texts he retained in his mind, Ananda answered, "82,000 from the Buddha and

2,000 from the brethren, making a total of 84,000 texts in all." Ananda's mind was a storehouse of Dharma knowledge; it can rightly be likened to a Buddhist library.

Devadatta, who was the Buddha's arch-enemy, had a plan to assassinate him. When Devadatta let loose a wild elephant with this wicked and murderous intention, Ananda tried to block the animal's path by throwing himself in front of the Enlightened One. Ananda was ready to sacrifice his own life rather than allow the Buddha to be attacked. Although the Buddha asked him thrice to step back, Ananda ignored this instruction. Using his supernatural powers, the Master protected Ananda and himself. This event illustrates that Ananda's devotion to the Buddha was genuinely selfless in nature.

Ananda did not mind spending his days under the shadow of the Buddha. Ananda was in fact a self-effacing monk even before attaining Arhatship; he never desired to upstage his mentor — the Buddha. Although Ananda associated closely with the Buddha and was aware of the latter's greatness, he was never envious of his Master. At no time did he regard himself as the Buddha's rival. The relationship between them was harmonious as it was based on mutual love and respect.

The Buddha, now almost eighty, was living his last days.

> *"I'm now at the end of my life*
> *And it is with difficulty that I can keep this body alive;*
> *I do so in the same way that one maintains a cart*
> *That is old and in a bad condition."*

Ananda was filled with sadness. Thereupon the Buddha said,

> *"Ananda, each one of you must be an island*
> *Unto yourself;*
> *Seek refuge only in yourself;*
> *Seek not refuge in anyone;*
> *Making the Dharma your island,*
> *Live in the Dharma which is your refuge;*
> *Seek not refuge in anyone."*

Once again the Awakened One was emphasising the importance of being utterly independent and self-reliant. The Dharma alone is enough for the intelligent person who has understood the uselessness of prayer, worship and such practices that are deeply rooted in the desire for help from external agencies.

Ananda held a doorjamb and started sobbing on learning from the Buddha that he would soon pass away.

"Don't weep, Ananda,
Don't feel sad," said the Buddha,
"Haven't I told you that all meetings
Must end in partings,
And also that everything, be it animate or inanimate,
Is impermanent and subject to change?
Over a long period, Ananda, you have looked after me
With a loving heart.
Try hard and attain Arhatship."

Turning to the monks, the Buddha proceeded to praise Ananda:

"Monks, Ananda has four noteworthy virtues.
What are they?
Monks wishing to see me meet Ananda first.
On meeting him they are pleased by the way he behaves;
When he converses with them, they are more pleased;
When he delivers a short discourse they like it;
And wish to hear more;
When Ananda remains silent;
It is a joy for them to see him;
In that quiet state."

Once when the Buddha was sojourning in Vesali, it being the rainy season, he told Ananda,

"The Tathagata could live
Until the end of this aeon,
Provided he is requested to do so."

But Ananda failed to make this specific request. The Buddha

made the same statement for the second and third time, even then Ananda, apparently failing to take the hint, remained quiet. He was silent in the sense that he did not request the Buddha to prolong his life until an aeon's end. Why did Ananda fail to take action despite the Buddha's remark that he would, if specifically requested, extend the duration of his life? Why, given Ananda's great sorrow at the Buddha's impending death, did Ananda fail to implore the Master to live longer? Perhaps he did not fully understand the Buddha's statement; perhaps he was absolutely dumfounded by the sorrowful news; perhaps his personal feelings towards the Buddha had temporarily clouded his mind. Was his mindfulness temporarily in abeyance?

At the First Council one of the several accusations made against Ananda was that he forgot to request the Master to continue living for an aeon. Many commentators have strongly criticised Ananda for his inaction. Such criticisms seem unjustified, considering the fact that Ananda had not yet attained Enlightenment, for he was then a mere stream-enterer, not a fully accomplished Arhat. In other words, he was not infallible in the sense that he was still prone to making mistakes.

The traditional explanation for his lapse is that poor Ananda was under the sway of Mara, the Evil One, who is seen both as an actual person (i.e. as a deity) and also as the personification of evil, passions, death, worldly existence, defilement, the Aggregates and the like. Mara would have had a vested interest in influencing Ananda's mind, thereby curtailing the Master's lifespan so that prospective disciples of the Buddha are prevented from escaping from Mara's grip. Expressed differently, Mara is keen on deterring people from aspiring to Nirvana.

Mara next confronted the Buddha and reminded him that 45 years ago, just after his Illumination, the Buddha had made him a promise. On that momentous occasion Mara had asked the Buddha to enter full Nirvana or Parinirvana, involving the death of the Perfect One, but the Buddha made it clear that his life would end only after he had taught and instructed people, and also after the Dharma had been established. Now that the Buddha had succeeded in those declared objectives, Mara reminded him that he must keep his promise and depart this life. The Buddha said,

> *"Evil One, don't worry yourself.*
> *Soon the Parinirvana of the Tathagata*
> *Will happen.*
> *After three months the Tathagata*
> *Is going to pass away."*

Then the Buddha gave up his will to live. At that very moment there was thunder and the earth shook and trembled. It was as though all nature were bemoaning the Buddha's forthcoming demise.

When Ananda inquired about the cause of the earthquake, the Buddha answered that there are eight reasons for the sudden shaking of the earth. First, earthquakes happen when great forces are in a state of movement; second, when persons with supernatural powers achieve high levels of meditation; the last six reasons are related to the conception, the birth, the Illumination, the setting in motion of the wheel of Dharma (*i.e.*, the teaching of the Dharma for the first time), the abandonment of the will to live; and lastly, the Parinirvana of a Buddha. Needless to say, the cosmic forces are in consonance with the spiritual culmination of Mother Nature — the attainment of Buddhahood.

One is reminded of what Shakespeare wrote in quite a different context:

> *"When beggars die, there are no comets seen;*
> *The heavens themselves blaze forth the death of princes."*
> — Julius Caesar

Truly, the heavens were blazing forth the imminent death of the Prince of princes — former Prince Siddhartha.

When the Buddha explained to Ananda that he had already told Mara that he would live only for another three months, Ananda earnestly asked him thrice to continue living for an entire aeon. Thereupon the Teacher said,

> *"Ananda, you were at fault.*
> *You were unable to understand*

The simple suggestion of the Tathagata,
And you failed to ask him to continue with his life.
Had you done so twice,
The Tathagata might have turned you down,
But he would have agreed —
Had you requested the third time."

The Buddha recalled that he had actually reminded Ananda fifteen times before that he could live for a whole aeon, but every time Ananda had not said anything.

The Buddha, in conclusion, delivered a discourse on the theme of impermanence.

"Have I not instructed from the outset
That everything that is near and dear
Is subject to change, separation and ending?
When anything arises, comes into existence,
It being conditioned and prone to decay,
None can prevent its destruction.
Besides, it is not possible for a Tathagata
Not to feel honour bound to keep his word —
After three months he shall attain Parinirvana."

Is it right and fair to blame Ananda? Even if we assume that Ananda had committed a terrible error by not requesting the Buddha to lengthen his life — Ananda was liable to err in the sense that he had not yet attained Perfection — it can be argued that the Buddha, out of compassion for mankind, could well have overlooked Ananda's so-called fault — and lived longer for the welfare and happiness of thousands who had not yet had the benefit of knowing the teachings directly and personally from the Master himself. It is difficult to understand why the Buddha's decision about whether or not to remain longer on earth was going to hinge solely on the request that Ananda was expected to make, but failed to do.

At the age of eighty the Buddha had fulfilled his mission in so far as he had not only taught the Dharma far and wide but also firmly established it via the orders for monks and nuns. His ailing body was frail. Maintaining his health was becoming problematic. Therefore the time was ripe for his demise. One gets the impression that he would have decided to die anyway, regardless of what Ananda would have said about the matter, especially because of his previous promise to Mara to pass away only after finishing his special work.

Ananda lived to the ripe old age of 120. He died between the banks of the Rohini river as two parties were in dispute over the right to own the entire relics. There was spontaneous combustion and the body burned, and in the process the relics fell down in equal amounts on the two sides of the river.

"Tranquil in mind,
Tranquil in speech,
Tranquil in action,
Liberated through true knowledge,
He has found perfect peace."

— Dhammapada, 96

"Not being credulous,
Who realises the Uncreated,
Whose cycle of births has ceased,
Gone beyond good and evil,
Who vomited out his desires,
He is supreme among men."

— Dhammapada, 97

"Delightful is the place
Where Arhats abide —
Village, the woods,
Land low or high."

— Dhammapada, 98

"Delightful are the forests
Wherein the earthbound
Cannot find any delight.
Not being pleasure-bound,
Arhats there do rejoice."

— Dhammapada, 99

2

Facing Death : Kisagotami's Problem

Sooner or later we have to accept the fact that all our relations, acquaintances, friends and loved ones are going to pass away. Having to come to terms with this sad fact will not be easy. But much more difficult will be resigning ourselves to the unpleasant truth that we ourselves will someday have to enter the house of death.

Numerous are our fears, such as the fear of darkness, the fear of snakes, spiders and other dangerous animals, the fear of losing our jobs and incomes, the fear of natural catastrophes such as floods and earthquakes. There are also our various unknown fears, but I think that the principal primordial fear in man is this fear of dying. Are we prepared to say goodbye to our bodies that we have looked after with great care?

Can we also let go of our attachments and psychological problems? Man is nothing but a bundle of attachments, traits, fears, frustrations, hopes, ambitions, likes, dislikes, resentments, petty jealousies, lurking pride and so forth. Can we let go of these tendencies now and eventually have a peaceful end? Can we die psychologically before dying physically? Can we, in other words, die before we die?

The story of Kisagotami causes one to have deep feelings for her sufferings. Born into a poverty-stricken family, the girl was lean and haggard (*kisa*). Gotami by clan, she was a kinswoman of Gotama the Buddha. Inwardly wealthy but outwardly poor and unattractive, finding a suitable husband for Kisa had become problematic. But her appearance, such as it was, did not deter a rich merchant from falling for her. He valued her great and noble qualities. They got married. Then the couple had to contend with the deep resentment of members his family towards Kisa. She felt uneasy about her situation. Her husband suffered from divided loyalties as he was attached to his parents and also to his dear wife Kisa.

When Kisa bore a son, her in-laws suddenly decided to accept her! Kisa was no longer ostracised by her husband's relations. At last she felt at peace with herself. There was, besides, the bond of affection between mother and child that helped her to calm down. She grew very attached to the boy, especially because the latter's birth had ensured her entry into her husband's family circle that had previously been hostile towards her.

But once the boy was old enough to run about and play games he fell ill and passed away. Poor Kisa was grief-stricken to such an extent that she became inconsolable. It was impossible for her to accept her tragic situation philosophically.

Kisa was having several worrisome problems. She thought, "Would my in-laws start hating me by thinking that my bad karma prevents me from begetting a son?", "Would they reject me now?' and "Would my husband find himself another wife?" Refusing to face the unpalatable tragedy that struck her, Kisa's mind started deluding herself. She believed that the boy was only ill and would soon be back to normal life if only the right medical remedy were found. Her fertile imagination preferred pure fantasy to accepting the pain of separation from her beloved boy.

When reality is hard to take, the mind is given to seeking refuge in illusion.

Carrying the corpse upon her hip, Kisa went from door to door at Savatthi. She went begging, "I need medicine for my boy." But the people said, "Isn't the child dead? Of what use is medicine?" Without taking no for an answer, the desperate woman would approach strangers and passers-by and make the same plea. Deep was her conviction that the child was only sick. Some poured scorn on Kisa. Soon she became an object of ridicule. Realising that Kisa was now a distraught woman, a kind-hearted man felt sympathy for her. He directed her to visit the Buddha.

Fortunately the Master was residing at the monastery of Anathapindika in Savatthi. Kisa lost no time in visiting him.

Still carrying the corpse in her arms, Kisa rushed to the Buddha as a last resort.

"Master," she implored him, "I need medicine for my son."

"Mustard seeds," said the Buddha. His remedy took those present by surprise. Those words raised her hopes. She was full of joy. Mustard seeds are not difficult to obtain. It seemed like an easy solution to a difficult problem. But the Buddha explained that Kisa must get mustard seeds on one condition — that the small amount of required mustard seeds must be obtained only from a home wherein no one had ever died.

Exuding confidence, Kisa went to the first house and made an urgent request for some mustard seeds.

"Sure," said the householder who proceeded to offer her some mustard seeds.

When the required seeds were offered her, Kisa posed the question, "but has any human being ever died in this house?"

"Yes," was the answer. It was a most disappointing response. Kisa realised that the condition laid down by the Buddha must be respected. It was absolutely necessary to get some mustard seeds *only* from a home that had *never* known death. She should, in other words, get the seeds only from a dwelling that had not been in any way contaminated by death. Kisa went from door to door, but she failed to find a house that had never been visited by Mara. Great was Kisa's sorrow. She remarked that far more persons were dead than those still alive.

At dusk it dawned on Kisa that death was inevitable. Whosoever is born must also die. That is the unalterable fate of every living being. That is the universal law. Her reluctance to acknowledge that her son had died was now a thing of the past.

Interestingly, when Kisagotami approached the Buddha, why did the Master choose not to preach a sermon on death, as was his wont? Instead of giving her verbal advice, he set her an assignment in the manner of a professor that involved fieldwork. Probably this was the only means of bringing the mentally deranged woman to her senses. At that time she lacked in mental calmness, which is preliminary to understanding a difficult discourse. The Buddha's solutions to problems were invariably tailored to the unique needs of specific individuals or specific groups.

Kisa went to meet the Buddha after she had buried her dead son in a cemetery. He then inquired whether she had managed to get the required mustard seeds.

"I don't need them, sir," Kisa replied, "only give me refuge." The Buddha thereupon declared:

"A great flood comes
And sweeps away a sleeping village.
In the same way, death comes
And carries off the man
Who dotes on his children and cattle,
And whose mind is enslaved by sensual pleasures"

— Dhammapada, 287

The Master's words made a profound impact on Kisa with the result that she attained the first of the four stages towards Enlightenment. She became a stream-enteret (*Sotapanna*). A stream-enterer will not only never again be reborn in lower worlds, but will also never be reborn more than seven times. The Buddha granted her request to become a nun. Following her higher ordination, Kisa devoted her time and energy to studying the Dharma.

Her day was fast drawing to a close. It was getting dark. As Kisa was watching the flickering flames of her oil lamp, it struck her that the quick and changing movements of the flames were similar to the seemingly ceaseless cycle of births and deaths. The Buddha was aware that Kisa was now ready for that ultimate breakthrough in her long search for Liberation. Therefore he visited her and made an important statement:

"One day's seeing
Of the deathless and unconditioned Nirvana

Is better than living for a hundred years
Without seeing it"

— Dhammapada 114

No sooner had Kisa heard the Buddha's words than she shed her lingering taints and became an Arhat.

The Buddha was addressing an assembly in the Jeta Grove. While referring to the strong points of various nuns, he declared that Kisa was foremost among the wearers of rough robes. He paid her a compliment by saying that Kisa excelled herself in ascetic practices. Thereupon Kisa, who was gratefully aware of her attainments, sang the following psalm in the Buddha's presence:

"The Sage has praised
Friendship with noble beings.
Even a fool who keeps
Their company becomes intelligent.

"Be with the worthy!
Thereby wisdom develops.
There will be freedom
From every sorrow.

"Observe how sorrow comes
And how it ends.
Observe the Eightfold Path
And the Four Noble Truths.

"Woman's lot is sorrowful,
Taught the Tamer of hearts.
Sharing home with co-wives is sorrowful,
Painful childbirth is also sorrowful.

"Some slit their babes' throats,
Poison the delicate take.
Stillbirth is sorrowful
When mother and child die.

"I walked up the Eightfold Path
That leads to the Deathless.

Nirvana I attained.
At the Mirror of the Dharma
I did gaze.
Healed is my hurt.
I have laid down my burden.
My task has been done.
My heart has found full
Liberation.
I, sister Kisa-Gotami,
Say this!"

One morning the Bhikkuni Kisagotami, taking her begging bowl and robe, went on her alms round in Savatthi. After her meal she sat under a tree in the Blind Men's Grove. When she was in meditation Mara, the Evil One, noticed her presence there. Wanting to instil fear into her and cause a disturbance, Mara started speaking to her, "now that your son is no more, why are you alone looking so sad? You who entered the woods unaccompanied, are you in search of a man?" The Evil One mocked her. Kisa pondered over the words she had just heard. She thought,

"Were these words uttered by a human being
Or a non-human one?
Ah, this is Mara
Who is hell-bent on frightening and disturbing me."

Nevertheless, Kisa decided to give answers to Mara's questions. Kisa said,

"The death of sons is long past.
No longer is there a search for men.
No longer is there sorrow.
No longer do I lament.
Nor am I frightened of you, friend."

By addressing Mara as 'friend', Kisagotami indicated that she had transcended the fear of dying. She was implying that she had attained the Deathless. Kisagotami proceeded to describe the nature of her inner Attainment:

> *"Craving is no more,*
> *Ignorance has been torn asunder.*
> *Having defeated Death,*
> *I live without impurities."*

Realising that Kisa fully understood Mara's ways and wiles, Mara felt very unhappy. He left the place immediately.

There is more to death than meets the eye. Death can teach us many lessons. Death is a reminder of the fundamental truth that there is nothing that is not subject to change, decay and demise. It is also a reminder of the related truth that we are only temporary residents in this world of transient things. A lover in the heat of the moment might promise eternal love, forgetting that all human ties are transitory.

The principle of transitoriness pervades all nature. A fig tree that one plants in a garden, for example, grows slowly and after a time it is in full leaf. Then it has delicious fruits. In the autumn the leaves change colour and fall. After its lifespan, the tree dies. Are we in any way different from this tree? Is there anything within us, either in our bodies or minds, that has the quality of permanency? Very deceitful is the mind. Out of its sense of insecurity born of transitoriness, the illusion-prone mind invents the idea of an eternal soul or an everlasting God! How the mind cherishes illusions! Illusions have no factual foundation but they are a great comfort to those in sorrow.

Any person who takes the trouble to observe the workings of his or her mind, which can be done by simply watching the thought process in action — simply seeing how all the time thoughts, feelings and sensations arise and disappear — will soon discover that the contents of the inner river are constantly changing. The river is in a state of perpetual flux. These contents or aggregates *(khandhas)* fall into five main categories — forms (*rupa*), sensations (*vedana*), perceptions (*sanna*), volitions (*sankhara*) and consciousness (*vinnana*). Is there anything that is unchanging and permanent in this quickly moving stream? The fleeting feelings, the darting thoughts and the volatile sensations, all of which suddenly surface and immediately disappear, like flashes of lightening, are like the millions of drops of water that are tossing about in a waterfall. In reality, what we call the 'waterfall' does not exist; it seems to be there, when in fact there are only countless drops of water in a state of movement. Similarly, the delusion of 'I' is apparent but not real. Those who care to observe the restless thought process will invariably realise its inherent impermanence. Understanding the impermanence of all things (*Anicca)* — their rising, changing, passing and disappearing from moment to moment — rarely happens, but if it does, one instantly has a deep insight into the unsubstantiality of all conditioned phenomena.

Understanding the truth about impermanence (*Anicca)* is the prelude to understanding the other profound truth that the 'I' or 'self' — this vague impression that lurks in the mind that 'I am' or 'I exist' — is nothing more than a mere concept. Like all mental images, the image of 'myself' emerges from time to time but has it an everlasting existence? In social life for the purpose of communication we have to use words such as 'me' or 'mine', whereas the 'I' or 'self', which is a cherished illusory belief, has no factual or real existence.

The Buddhist doctrine of *Anatta* and animism ('anima' in Latin is 'soul') are diametrically opposed, since animism is based on the belief that all natural objects and the universe has a soul; there is also the belief that these souls are capable of existing outside their material bodies.

There are, alas, many theists and Hindus who have invested the self with the quality of immortality. It is their vain attempt to immortalise something in a changing situation wherein nothing is immortal. The doctrine of 'impersonality', or 'non-self' 'non-ego' or 'absence of ego' (*Anatta*) is one of the principal pillars on which the Dharma is founded. Either within the mind-body or outside it, is there anything that has an abiding substance? Is there a soul or an eternal ego-entity either within us or without?

The mere intellectual comprehension of the illusory nature of the self is not enough. It will be a great pity if this teaching is relegated to the level of a mere concept or theory. But when there is a profound understanding of the truth that the self is non-existent, the flower of virtue will suddenly be in full bloom.

So long as the sense of self even subtly survives in the mind, one's thoughts, words and deeds will be coloured by selfishness. However, there will be selflessness with the cessation of the stingy and acquisitive self. Instead of the prevalence of selfishly calculated acts of so-called giving, there will be genuine generosity (*Dana).* It is the ego that likes to strengthen itself by grabbing various possessions. But the ego-free person does not feel the need to own anything: there is no self that says "I must have this or that". He is free from craving (*Tanha*), which is the main cause of suffering and the continuation of the chain of recurrent births.

When selfishness is dropped, in the ensuing state of purity there will be both loving-kindness (*Metta*) and compassion *(Karuna).* The one who has discarded all sense of self will not feel insulted when people are rude to him or when he is the victim of abusive or offensive language, and by the same token he will not be proud when he is showered with praise. Such a person is free of ego oriented pride (*Asmi-Mana*).

Above all, the sage who has transcended the self is free from suffering (*Dhukkha*). Never again will he or she be liable to suffering on account of the exalted state of inner purity or taintlessness.

> *"There is no fire akin to lust,*
> *There is no seizer akin to anger,*
> *There is no net akin to delusion,*
> *There is no river akin to craving."*
>
> — Dhammapada, 251

3

Recipe for a Happy Society

The Buddha's recipe for a happy society can be found in the *Sigalovada Sutta*. He was concerned for the welfare, prosperity, progress and peace of society. He delivered a long discourse on aspects of social life that are applicable to all societies both ancient and modern. All the interesting points he made about living harmoniously are timelessly true, which is a common feature of all his discourses.

In a sense this sutta can be described as a detailed code of conduct or behaviour.

The sermon was specifically aimed at laypersons and not renunciants. There is, incidentally, a certain symbiotic relationship between laypersons and renunciants in all Buddhist societies. Monks and nuns are not required to work for their livelihood. Laypersons provide monks and nuns with alms, who in return are regarded as the natural religious teachers of society. As a general rule renunciants are fit for that role as they are, or should be, relatively well versed in the Dharma.

When mendicants beg for food, going from house to house, they are expected not to cause any inconvenience to alms donors. This is a very delicate matter that must be handled sensitively and with discretion. They must be like the bee and their behaviour should not involve intrusion:

> *"As the bee*
> *Without injuring the flower, its colour or scent,*
> *Moves off after collecting nectar,*
> *In this manner the sage lives in his village."*
>
> — Dhammapada, 49

Sigalaka, the son of a householder, used to rise early and go from Rajagaha with his wet clothes and wet hair and pay homage to the different directions. He would do so with folded hands in the worshipping posture of a devotee. It must have been a touching sight at dawn.

In the *Atharva Veda* there is a spell to prevent bad things from happening from different directions. Worshipping the directions was a very ancient practice. It probably sprang into existence from the superstitious belief that it was an effective means of casting off ill-luck. Those who practised this morning ritual obviously derived an enormous sense of security and peace of mind. Many so-called religious ceremonies are considered as precious merely because they make people feel safe from danger, disease and various misfortunes.

The whole sutta is about the *right* way of worshipping the directions. I use the word 'worship' not literally but solely in its figurative sense. Instead of worshipping, or respectfully bowing before the directions, the Buddha advises Sigalaka that worshipping consists in leading a righteous life — there are a host of moral things to be done and a host of immoral things that must not be done. The Vedic ritual of worshipping the directions was completely meaningless to the Buddha. Nevertheless, understanding the traditional mindset of Sigalaka, the Master used the form of the ritual when delivering the discourse, but its deeper meaning and substance was entirely new and totally different from the way it had been traditionally regarded for centuries.

One morning as the Buddha was entering Rajagaha for alms he observed dripping wet Sigalaka in the act of worshipping the various quarters — the East, the South, the West, the North, the Nadir and the Zenith. When the Buddha asked him why he was worshipping the quarters, Sigalaka said, "I was instructed to do so by my father when he was dying. I do so out of respect for my father's words that I revere, honour and regard as sacred."

When the Buddha disapproved of these practices, Sigalaka requested the Teacher to show him the noble or Aryan way to pay homage to the *six directions.*

Defilements of Action

The Buddha asked the young householder to give up the four

defilements of action — the destruction of life, stealing, sexual misbehaviour and making untrue statements.

Evil Action

One should root out the four factors that result in evil action — attachment, ill will, delusion and fear.

Loss of Wealth

What are the *six ways* of losing wealth, which one must *not* follow?

First, the taking of intoxicants will result in dangers that are *sixfold* — the loss of wealth, the increase in disputes, bad health, the ruin of one's reputation, immodest behaviour and the lessening of intelligence.

Second, by strolling the streets at improper times, what will be the *sixfold* dangers? One is in a vulnerable situation and defenceless, and so are one's spouse and children, including one's property, one may have to bear the blame for others' misdeeds, unfounded malicious rumours about one would circulate, and one has to contend with all manner of problems.

Third, what are the *sixfold* dangers from going to shows and fairs? One always thinks — Where can one enjoy dancing? Where can one hear singing? Where can one hear music? Where can one hear recitations? Where can one hear the music of cymbals? Where can one hear drumming?

Fourth, what are the *sixfold* dangers in gambling? The winner becomes an object of hate, the loser laments his loss, there is a waste of wealth, the gambler remains a distrusted person in assemblies, his friends and associates much dislike him, and a gambler is seen as someone without the means to support a wife.

Fifth, what are the *sixfold* dangers in having bad friends? Any gambler, any libertine, any drunkard, any swindler, any impostor or any overbearing person becomes his companion.

Sixth, what are the *sixfold* dangers in the disposition to idleness? He does not do his work because he thinks 'it is too cold', 'it is too hot', 'it is too early', 'it is too late', 'I am too hungry' or 'I am too full'. Because he lives with these excuses, his duties remain undone, he acquires no wealth; and that which he already has, diminishes.

False Friends

The following *four* categories of persons should be regarded as false friends: a selfishly rapacious person who takes everything that he can, a man who merely talks, a person who is given to flattering others and one whose deeds result in losses.

What are the *four* reasons why a selfishly rapacious person, who takes all, has to be regarded as a false friend? He grabs everything for himself, he takes much and offers little, it is out of fear that he does his duties and he is self-seeking.

What are the *four* reasons why one who merely talks is a false friend? He talks about past favours, and future favours, he makes empty promises to get your favour, but when something is needed he says that much to his regret he cannot help.

What are the *four* reasons why a flatterer is a false friend? He condones one's wrong deeds. He disapproves of one's good deeds. He sings your praises to your face, but is given to backbiting.

What are the *four* reasons why a person whose deeds result in losses has to be regarded as a false friend? He is a companion when one is taking intoxicants, when one is strolling the streets during improper hours, when one is frequenting fairs and shows, and when one is gambling.

Loyal Friends

What are the *four* types who can be regarded as loyal friends? One who is helpful. One who is the same in weal and woe. One who is a good counsellor. One who is compassionate.

In what *four* ways is a loyal friend helpful? He guards you when you are inattentive, he protects your property when you are inattentive, he shelters you from danger, and offers twice what is requested when you are in need.

In what *four* ways is a loyal friend the same in weal and woe? He reveals to you his secrets. He conceals your secrets. He does not desert you in bad times. He is prepared to sacrifice his life for you.

In what *four* ways is a loyal friend a good counsellor? He restrains you from wrongdoing. He persuades you to do good. He provides information about things that you do not know. He shows you the direction of heaven.

In what *four* ways is a loyal friend compassionate? He does not take delight in your misery. He is very happy about the good things that happen to you. He restrains those who say bad things about you. He approves of those who speak well of you.

The wise person should devote himself to the aforesaid *four* kinds of friends, cherishing them as a mother cherishes her own child.

He should divide his wealth into four parts: one part is for his own use, two parts are for his work, and the last is saved for a rainy day.

Young householder, how must a noble disciple worship the *six* directions? The *six* directions are the following:

The *East* should be looked upon as the *parents.*
The *West* should be looked upon as the *wife and children.*
The *South* should be looked upon as the *teachers.*
The *North* should be looked upon as *friends and companions.*
The *Nadir* should be looked upon as *servants and workers.*
The *Zenith* should be looked upon as *ascetics and Brahmins.*

Mother and Father

What are the *five* ways in which a *son* must serve and help his *parents* as the *Eastern direction*?

I will support my parents who once supported me. I will serve and help them. I will be worthy of my family tradition. I will be worthy of what I inherit. I will offer alms in the name of my departed parents.

What are the *five* ways in which *parents* will reciprocate the services and help of their *son*?

They will deter him from wrongdoing. They will persuade him to be good. He is taught a skill. They will arrange for him a suitable wife, and at the right time he will get a legacy from them. Thus the *Eastern direction* is covered — it is made peaceful and free from danger.

Husband and Wife

What are the *five* ways in which a *husband* should serve and help his *wife* as the *Western direction*? He honours her. He does not disparage her. He is faithful to her. He delegates authority to her. He gives her ornaments.

What are the *five* ways in which a *wife* will reciprocate the services and help of her *husband*? She works well. She is hospitable to the relations and the folk around. She is faithful to him. She protects the belongings. She is careful and efficient in her work. Thus the *Western direction* is covered — it is made peaceful and free from danger.

Teachers

What are the *five* ways in which a *student* should serve and help his *teachers* as the *Southern direction*? He greets them by deferentially rising from his seat. He waits on them. He listens to them attentively with an eagerness to learn. He looks after them. He learns the skills that they teach.

What are the *five* ways in which *teachers* will reciprocate the services and help of their *student*? They instruct him well. They make sure that the student has understood the lessons well. They instruct him in all the skills. They recommend him to their friends and associates. They provide him with security in every direction. Thus the *Southern direction* is covered — it is made peaceful and free from danger.

Friends and Companions

What are the *five* ways in which a *person* must serve and help his *friends and companions* as the *Northern direction*? He gives gifts. He speaks with them courteously. He serves them well. He treats them unselfishly. He fulfils his promises.

What are the *five* ways in which *friends and companions* reciprocate the services and help of this *person*? They will protect him and look after him when he is inattentive. They will safeguard his property when he is inattentive. They will be shelters in any dangerous situation. They will not abandon him in bad times. They will be considerate towards his wife and children.

Thus the *Northern direction* is covered — it is made peaceful and free from danger.

Servants and Workers

What are the *five* ways in which a *master* must serve and help his *servants and workers* as the *Nadir*? He must assign them work according to their strength or ability. He must provide them with nourishment and pay. He must look after them when they are sick. He should share special delicacies with them. He must release them from the burden of work at the right time.

What are the *five* ways in which *servants and workers* reciprocate the services and help of the *master*? They will get up before the master. They retire after him. They do not take anything dishonestly. They work well. They maintain his good reputation.

Thus the *Nadir* is covered — it is made peaceful and free from danger.

Ascetics and Brahmins

What are the *five* ways in which a man must serve and help *ascetics and Brahmins* as the *Zenith*? By compassionate deeds, by compassionate speech and compassionate thoughts, by welcoming them at all times, and by providing them with their material needs.

What are the *six* ways in which *ascetics and Brahmins* reciprocate the services and help of the *layperson*?

They will prevent him from doing evil. They will urge him to do good. They will feel great compassion for him. They will teach him what he does not know. They will clarify what they have already taught. They will direct him heavenward.

Thus the *Zenith* is covered — it is made peaceful and free from danger.

Sigalaka the householder, who was obviously overjoyed to hear this long discourse, which the Buddha had specially delivered for his benefit, exclaimed, "Wonderful, Exalted One, wonderful! It is as if someone has straightened what had been bent, or uncovered what had been hidden, or has shown the way to the lost, or has brought an oil-lamp that dispels darkness so that those with eyes can see. In this way the Buddha has expounded the Teaching! I take refuge in the Buddha, the Dharma and the Sangha. May the Exalted One accept me as a lay-follower from today until the end of my days!"

****

"There is no fire akin to lust,
No defect akin to hatred,
No sorrow akin to the body
No happiness higher than Peace."

— Dhammapada, 202

"When confronted by death,
Sons cannot protect you against it,
Nor father and relations.
No kinsman can snatch you out of the jaws of death."

— Dhammapada, 288

"Understanding this fact, the wise and virtuous
Should remove the obstacles to Nirvana."

— Dhammapada, 289

4

The Joy of Solitude

Sacred literature is replete with significant instances of serious seekers who felt strongly that they must sooner or later answer their inner call and become hermits.

The accumulation of worldly goods no longer held any attraction for real recluses; they lost all interest in mundane matters; disillusioned with exciting diversions and passing pleasures, they shunned social life and sought solitude instead.

The Quaker poet Mary Mollineux (1651-95) expressed herself exultantly in the following words:

> *"How sweet is harmless solitude!*
> *What can its joys control?*
> *Tumults and noise may not intrude,*
> *To interrupt the soul."*

One can of course probe the mind and heart anywhere. It can be done even in a crowded market place with men, women and children bustling in and out of shops. But self-inquiry or the inward journey is best done in moments of solitude.

What joy is it to be all alone in a secluded place that is undisturbed by people or the deafening roar of traffic! What a bliss to take solitary walks along the seashore or in the silent woods and commune with Mother Nature!

Silence and solitude are rare and precious commodities. The saints and sages of yore set great store on both silence and solitude. Monks and nuns dwelling in monasteries, and persons of no fixed abode, they have all tended to select silent places for meditation.

It is of course possible to observe oneself even in crowded railway compartments or noisy discotheques, but meditation is easiest in surroundings without disturbing noises.

Those devoted to religious contemplation have always been drawn to peaceful places with a certain idyllic calm. They have liked the noise-free serene summits of mountains with panoramic views of the valleys below, which symbolise the superior solitary life of the recluse that is in contradistinction to the mundane existence of the vast majority living on the plains.

Religious contemplatives have also liked quiet and secluded caves as well as isolated sea shores with prana-rich soothing breezes, wherefrom they could gaze at the endless horizons and contemplate the incalculable immensity of infinity and the nature of nothingness.

When recluses take refuge near rivers they can, while observing the changing and moving waters, contemplate on the universal truth about *Anicca*. They will see how the ripples on the surface of the waters constantly appear and disappear. Understanding the truth about the waters that are in a state of flux will supplement the understanding of the great inner truth about the flux of our own thoughts, feelings, emotions, sensations and the like that are also in a stream-like process. Nothing remains the same for everything changes from moment to moment. Every observable thing, both within ourselves and without, arises and stays for a while and vanishes. Everything that is formed must disintegrate sooner or later. Is there anything that is permanent?

We all know that the Bodhisattva, prior to attaining Enlightenment, had been meditating under the shade of that famous Bodhi Tree. As we ponder over that momentous event, it might strike us that he had been meditating not only in silence but also in solitude.

In *The Udana* there is an interesting description of an event, which illustrates that the Buddha set a high value on solitude.

Once the Buddha was staying at the Ghosita monastery near Kosambi. It was a time when he was not comfortable. During this uneasy period he was hemmed in by eight groups of persons — monks and nuns, men and women disciples, kings and royal ministers, and by sectarian gurus and their followers.

Then it occurred to him that

"I am at present hemmed in
By these groups of persons,
Hence I am uncomfortable
And not relaxed.
Suppose I were to live in seclusion,
Live away from these people?"

In the forenoon the Perfect One, after wearing his robe and taking his bowl and outer cloak, proceeded to Kosambi for almsfood. After having had his meal, he made sure that his lodging was neat and tidy. Once again he took his bowl and outer cloak and left the place. He walked away alone. Before leaving, neither did he inform his attendant about it nor did he take leave of the monks. He was not accompanied by anyone when he walked by stages until he arrived at Parileyyaka. There he stayed in a forest under a Sal tree.

Probably it was purely coincidental that a certain elephant had also become the victim of trying circumstances. The unpleasant situation in which the elephant had been placed was not basically different from that of the Buddha.

The elephant had been hemmed in by a crowd of male and female elephants, elephant calves and sucklings. He had to eat blades of grass with their tips taken off, and the other elephants ate the branches that he himself had broken down. Besides, he had to drink dirty water, and when he tried to wade across the water, the female elephants would push and knock against him. He was uncomfortable and not relaxed. Then it occurred to him, "suppose I were to live in seclusion, live away from them?"

The elephant left the herd and went to Parileyyaka. He approached the Buddha who was under the Sal tree. The elephant removed the grass from the spot that the Buddha was occupying. The elephant next used its trunk and brought drinking water for the Buddha.

While the Master was living there in seclusion and away from people, it occurred to him that

"Previously I was hemmed in
By groups of people,
And I was uncomfortable
And not relaxed."

Similarly, it occurred to the elephant that "previously I was hemmed in by a crowd of elephants, and I was uncomfortable and not relaxed, but now I am no longer hemmed in by them. I eat unbroken grass and the other elephants do not eat the branches that I have broken down. I drink fresh water and I am no longer jostled by female elephants. Now I live in comfort and I am relaxed."

The Buddha, seeing his own state of aloneness, and knowing the elephant's thoughts, was then inspired to say some words:

"The mind of the Noble One
And the mind of the noble elephant
Are in harmony,
The noble elephant
With long pole-like tusks
Who in the forest
Finds joy in solitude."
"The monk who has retreated to a lonely place,
Whose mind is quiet,
Who is clear about the Dharma,
Experiences a delight transcending that of men."

— Dhammapada, 373

"Should you find a thoughtful companion
Who is suitable for living with you,
Who is well-behaved and wise,
Live with him with joy
And mindfully avert all dangers."

— Dhammapada, 328

"Should you fail to find a thoughtful companion
Who is suitable for living with you,
Who is well-behaved and wise,
Then like a king,
Who leaves behind a conquered kingdom,

You should live alone like an elephant in the forest."

— Dhammapada, 329

"It is preferable to live alone.
With a fool no companionship is possible.
Walk alone with few wants,
Doing no harm,
In the manner of an elephant in the forest."

— Dhammapada, 330

5

Glimpses of Nothingness

Stargazing or observing the stars at night can be great fun. There is a widespread view that one cannot enjoy stargazing without having a rudimentary knowledge of astronomy. This is not true. It is not absolutely necessary to know the names of the numerous stars and planets in order to appreciate the splendour of the skies. All that is needed is a certain feeling for the mysterious beauty of the heavens. Similarly, a knowledge of botany is not indispensable for taking an absorbing interest in the thousands of flowers, shrubs and trees that one sees when wandering the woods.

Some are inclined to believe that stargazing is a harmless eccentricity. I have heard it said that it is a time-wasting hobby. Be that as it may, those who are given to stargazing know that it is its own reward.

I have long been accustomed to rising very early. I get out of bed around four o'clock every morning, and immediately afterwards I get out onto the spacious balcony that adjoins the room where I sleep. I do so regardless of whether the weather is good or not. It does not matter if it is windy, rainy or snowy. Then standing akimbo I love to survey the heavens. If it is not cloudy, one can see numerous shining stars. What a wonderful view! The sight of Venus, Jupiter, Mars, Mercury or Saturn in the sky gives me a thrill. I think that it is from about this time that the morning star can be seen in all its brilliance and beauty. It dominates the sky. Isn't it the happy herald of yet another day?

Throughout my life I have been seeing moving lights at night.

I have never fully understood the significance of these happenings. I have been noticing these moving lights at various times but not too often. When I was a child I used to have these experiences frequently, about once every three months. Now I have them only about twice each year. Have I become less perceptive with the passage of time?

It is only when I least expect to see these moving lights that I succeed in seeing them! In other words, they only appear unexpectedly. If I were to gaze up at the skies with the intention of seeing them, the chances of success are nil. In a sense it is somewhat disappointing that the moving stars are so elusive that they do not, as it were, present themselves whenever I am very keen on catching a glimpse of them!

Most of the day I sit at my desk where I either read or write. When the weather is fine I do some gardening or enjoy walking in the woods. But what I like best is doing nothing! Watching the drifting clouds in the vast blue skies of the Provence is an excellent form of relaxation. It can also be a marvellous sadhana. Gazing into space quietens down the mind, especially if there is a tendency towards mental hyperactivity.

Probably the best time for meditation is when the resplendent morning star is slowly emerging in the east. During the great stillness of the night I look at the bright stars in the pitch-black skies and pay my respects to Mother Nature, especially by admiring and adoring the marvellous heavens. Just being filled with a sense of wonder is in itself a valuable sadhana. The beauty of nature has a magical effect on me. Merely being aware of the incalculable immensity of space, and also being sadly conscious of the fact that the mind cannot comprehend its origin and mystery, results in a certain humiliating sense of inadequacy.

Whereas I used to regard myself as a person of some importance in the little world wherein I lived and worked, now I realise, having seen a small portion of the millions of sparkling stars in the skies, that I am really nothing more than a very tiny and insignificant speck of dust in the immense universe. This means that, if my body were to disintegrate and disappear, my demise would be of little consequence, just like a falling raindrop that permeates through the ground and is forgotten forever.

There was a time, much to my regret, when I viewed everything from the standpoint of my insatiable ego. How the ego always wanted to be the cynosure of the world's eyes! My self-centredness had created a complicated mass of prejudices, aversions and greed which, in turn, had caused a strengthening of the self.

One morning, while gazing into space, I was also watching my express train of thoughts and feelings, observing the seemingly endless procession of thoughts and feelings, simply seeing how thoughts and feelings arise and how they all end up in a misty nothingness. Then something strange happened. No, I did not make a remarkable breakthrough in the sense that this train suddenly stopped moving, but I found that some part of the ancient structure of the self started collapsing. There came into existence a new outlook on life that was both refreshing and rare. Ecstasy surged through me. I was high-spirited. I was filled with a certain selfless concern for the happiness and welfare of all beings. However, I understood very clearly that having a lot of compassion was certainly not the end of the spiritual journey. I realised that there was still a very long way to go to find that full and final Perfection.

On one occasion my wife Claudia and I had an unforgettable experience several years ago. It was very cold and the temperature was well below freezing point that wintry night sometime in December or January. We had just returned by train to Les Arcs-sur-Argens from a trip to Marseille. We started climbing the hill leading to our home, and next we were about to pass the house of Monsieur Jacques Bousquet, who was a retired gentleman and a friend of ours who sometimes visited us. He used to drop in for a chat. We all used to enjoy having tea together.

What I am going to describe happened a little past midnight while we were walking. We suddenly saw in front of us a strange bright light. The light was going slowly from left to right, moving in a semicircle over the roof of Mr Bousquet's house. Then it disappeared from sight. We were somewhat puzzled as to why we saw this moving light. Two weeks after this event our dear friend Monsieur Bousquet passed away.

Is it that a celestial being was trying to communicate with us? Was it a guardian angel attempting to warn us about what to expect soon? Was it an indication of his impending demise? We can never be sure of the special meaning, if any, of this mysterious light.

When I was a schoolboy way back in the 50s I used to spend the evenings walking on the sandy beaches near Colombo. There one can see some enchanting sunsets. The sky becomes a kaleidoscope of changing colours. The silhouettes of fishing catamarans against the crimson sky would enhance the beauty of the departing day. The birds return to their roosts. The cawing of crows becomes music to one's ears and is no longer a noisy disturbance. In the tropics it becomes dusky very quickly. Then after nightfall several friends and I would sit down on a rock bordering the beach. We would relish chatting for hours.

I would, on occasion, notice a shining light arching into the night sky and suddenly dipping below the Indian Ocean. The brilliant light somehow seemed like a luminous lantern light. It would curve very slowly towards the water and disappear therein. None of my friends would notice it. Whenever I tried to draw the attention of my friends to the moving light, they would either ignore me or say that I had been daydreaming .For this reason I stopped referring to the existence of these lights. In retrospect, it is such a pity that I could not share these experiences with my friends.

I have a happy recollection of a similar experience during my schooldays. For nearly one week the Sri Lankan author Dr E.W. Adikaram and I were the guests of the Indian philosopher U.G. Kṛishnamurti at the latter's home in Chennai or Madras as it was then called. His residence was in close proximity to the international headquarters of the Theosophical Society at Adyar. Every night after dinner these two learned gentlemen, who were considerably older than me, would sit on the veranda and have long philosophical discussions, which I thought were rather boring. I would sit all alone under a mango tree and either while away the time or enjoy stargazing. On several nights I saw star-like lights slowly flying up into the sky and then making a descent over the treetops. The tall coconut and palmyra palms sometimes blocked my view. These were all exciting experiences. When I gave detailed descriptions of the moving stars to these two friends, they dismissed them as trivial.

Once they had a good laugh. "You've been seeing fireflies", they remarked. Thereafter I kept quiet as I did not want to make a fool of myself.

I could never afford a high-powered telescope, let alone a radio telescope, yet one of the marvellous things I have seen with the naked eye is Halley's Comet with its spectacularly long tail which was fully visible for several days here in the South of France. Thank goodness our skies are very clear on most days during the year. The appearance of this comet, which happens rarely, was fortunately well publicised in the press.

How thrilling when there are momentary lines of light in the sky caused by shooting stars or meteors! Those sudden streaks of light are so impressive as though they are emanating from a celestial display of fireworks. Whereas shooting stars or meteors move extremely quickly, like flashes of lightning, and are also of very short duration — just a few hurried seconds, the moving lights described in here travel gracefully and slowly like a bird on the wing.

Once I was the recipient of hate mail. An angry American reader of one of my books strongly disagreed with some of my philosophical views, and he proceeded to send me an abusive letter. He even wrote that I would be rendering a service to the world by giving up writing altogether. Believing that the man was emotionally disturbed, the best course of action seemed to forgive and forget. So at first I accepted the situation, and I did not lose my composure, particularly because I believed that every writer must sooner or later expect to receive from his readers not only bouquets but also brickbats. But when this reader continued sending several such offensive letters I started harbouring some resentment against him. Agitated, I had a few sleepless nights.

One night it convincingly occurred to me that my mind was neither peaceful nor clean as it was stained with resentment. There was then, in other words, an honest awareness of my troubled state of mind. That realisation immediately resulted in the riddance of resentment. The hitherto restless and revengeful mind became calm and unburdened. I suddenly changed without ever having made any effort to do so. My feelings of hostility towards that reader were instantaneously replaced by friendly feelings towards him.

Happily I opened the door and went to the adjacent balcony to have some fresh air. At that very moment a small but powerful light arched over the garden right in front of me. I knew at gut level that my new state of inward purity was meeting with the approval of an invisible celestial being. What an extraordinary experience!

In Sri Lanka such phenomenal lights are termed *Devata Eli* which means 'celestial lights'. The *Devas* or celestial beings are given to visiting and honouring only those whose lives are characterised by an emphasis on virtue, compassion and meritorious deeds. The *Devas* provide such persons with protection. By the same token, the *Devas* keep away from degenerates and all those whom they consider to be impure.

I was feeling very tired. As I wanted to go to bed I locked the balcony door and returned to my room. To my surprise, the air inside the room had the sweet smell of jasmine.

****

"Others' faults are easily noticed,
But one's own are difficult to see.
We winnow others' faults,
But hide our own,
Like a wicked fowler who hides himself."
— Dhammapada, 252

"The one who observes the faults of others,
And is ever taking offence,
In him the taints grow.
He is nowhere near the termination of taints."
— Dhammapada, 253

6

Why Worry about Growing Old?

My dear Gerda,

It is nice of you to pose some stimulating questions about old age. Some people are at their best when they are challenged. As for me, every challenge forces me to think deeply. I feel compelled to rack my brains, but even so I do not always succeed in finding the right answers. Any question that results in turning our attention inward, instead of outwards, is good and desirable as it is bound to promote self-examination. The mind is a land that has to be explored all the time, otherwise there is the possibility of the mind being under various delusions. Like weeds and thorny bushes, which spring up on jungle footpaths that are not frequently trodden, various prejudices and misconceptions cloud our judgements whenever there is no self-observation. Therefore we can come to the safe conclusion that the best guarantee of sanity is self-examination throughout one's entire life, particularly during old age when the mind is replete with memories.

What is the crux of the whole problem of growing old? The ageing process goes on all the time until we die. Can anyone permanently or even temporarily halt this movement? It is beyond our control. We have no choice but to accept the fact that ageing is inevitable. Since I have to resign myself to the fact that I am no longer a young man, I am not embarrassed about my grey hair. I am not ashamed of the fine lines on my face. But a problem will surely arise if I try to change my appearance with the intention of concealing my real age. If I try to look like an adolescent I will not only be trying to deceive the world but also be wasting money on cosmetic surgery or make-up.

Society, no doubt, categorises me as an 'aged person', but in truth I do not regard myself as either 'young' or 'old'. All I know is that my body is constantly changing. The body changes from moment to moment, change goes on ceaselessly, extending over our entire lifespan. Ageing does not begin at 55, 60 or 65 as is widely believed. A one-week-old baby is old in comparison with a baby who has just been born. Our concept of age arises only because the human mind is given to comparing and contrasting. If I stop remembering my age, if I cease seeing myself as a man of lesser importance in society merely because of my advancing years, can I not avoid much unhappiness? When the sense of agedness is replaced by the sense of agelessness, our present joylessness will go into eclipse and there will be a state of inner peace and contentment.

Are animals aware of their age? Are animals quick to take offence if other animals forget their birthdays? Do they worry about growing old? Many old persons, either because they are very lonely or because they find it nearly impossible to make friends, keep pets who become good companions, but little do human beings realise that they can learn a lot from their cats, dogs and other domestic animals.

What is your role model for the period of your old age?

On account of the deep conviction that creativity best expresses itself only when it is untrammelled, I could never bring myself to model my behaviour on that of someone else. I have, no doubt, been inspired and influenced by the lives and teachings of the really great such as the Buddha, Socrates and Ramana Maharshi; even so I dislike becoming a copy of any person. The one who makes himself a replica of another person only stifles his uniqueness. This is true in all spheres of life. For example, no writer worth his salt would ever want to copy the style of another author.

After working as a librarian in various libraries in England and Australia over a period of 26 years, I took early retirement at the age of 52. There was no great contrast between my working life and my retired life in the sense that there was no sudden change from one stage of life to another. Actually there was hardly any change. This means that there was no dramatic alteration in my way of life. Neither did my healthy lifestyle change nor did my standard of living fall at all. I mention this fact because nowadays many pensioners, on account of their reduced income following retirement, sadly find that they can no longer live in comfort. They are unfortunately not free from financial worries.

I had been a part-time writer for 26 years, whereas after retirement I became a full-time author who, luckily, is no longer interrupted by the obligation to earn his living. I feel no need to model myself on anyone after retirement as I am simply continuing to be what I have always been — a writer. There are, though, some noteworthy differences between my previous state of slavery and my present state of freedom.

I was very happy when the state gave me permission to retire. It was as though I had finished serving a long and painful prison sentence! After a quarter of a century of languishing in prison, I was about to be released! At first I could not believe that this was really going to happen. With a sigh of relief I said to myself, "Never again will I be treated like a dog by heartless employers! Never again will they be able to hurl racist abuse at me! Never again would anyone dare to breathe down my neck!" I think that nearly all my bosses, with the possible exception of about one or two kind-hearted gentlemen, were bullies and sadists. It truly gladdened my heart that I will henceforth be my own boss.

On weekdays I am no longer required to clock on at 9 a.m. and clock off at 5 p.m. Nowadays I take siestas after lunch, whereas during my working life I used to sit at my office desk in front of an opened book and, while pretending to read it, I would, feeling very fatigued, have an undisturbed doze! If I slept for more than 30 minutes, the chief librarian, who was a strict disciplinarian, would gently tap on my shoulder and say, "Wake up!" Once the boss was so drunk that he himself fell asleep in the afternoon. Some members of staff, including myself, seized the opportunity for forty winks!

It is a pity that many start leading inactive lives after retirement. I do not belong to this category as I am more active now than during the time when I was part of the workforce. How wonderful that there is now a noticeable increase in the amount of reading and writing that I do! On the other hand, fortunately, there is now an easy tempo of life. I am happy to be working at a leisurely pace. I have known several retirees who had heart attacks because they failed to slow down a bit in their old age.

I was acquainted with several elderly retirees whom I shall describe briefly. They were well-to-do, yet inwardly poor insofar as they were totally *unaware* of the reasons or various influences underlying their deeds. So I felt that they were not worthy of emulation. I could not possibly model myself on the following typically aged persons.

There was this aged Australian neighbour of mine, a tall and hefty man with an amiable manner, who loved to spend his nights watching pornographic video cassettes. He was *unaware* that he was vicariously reliving his early years of promiscuity. Once he invited me to see such a movie in his flat. When I remarked that it was high time he outgrew his animalistic urges, the man simply laughed at me and said that I was 'a total nutcase'.

I also knew an Australian widow whose only interest in life was looking after her many grandchildren. All her money and energies were devoted to this purpose. There is no gainsaying that her good deeds benefitted these children and also relieved the burden on their parents. Nevertheless, this lady was escaping from herself insofar as she was *unaware* of the fact that she was not only vicariously reliving her childbearing years but also giving expression to her maternal feelings. She was *unaware* of the operation of these strong currents within her. That awareness, had it existed, would have made her a person with a healthy detachment from the world. There is nothing particularly wrong in having maternal feelings, provided one is not only aware of the existence of these feelings, but also have these maternal feelings with a sense of detachment from the world.

Only deeds that are done with disinterestedness and detachment are pure and spiritual. But actions that spring from one's psychological needs are impure, although others might benefit from such deeds. Which is better, receiving a gift from a giver who is psychologically impure, or receiving one that is given with pure affection?

When I was living in Switzerland I knew an aged man with an immense fortune. He was so obsessively attached to his money that he became suspicious of people, fearing that they might cheat him out of his money. Consequently he had hardly any friends.

He loved playing chess as it was an intellectually challenging game; but, more importantly, chess helped him to develop strategies for dealing with people who might have designs on his vast income.

This short, bald and stoutly built man, who had some resemblance to Picasso in appearance but lacked the latter's artistic genius, spent much time watching football on TV, thereby vicariously enjoying the spirit of competitiveness and combativeness that are implicit in all such sports as well as in the world of commerce. This elderly and respectable Swiss gentleman was certainly a genius at selling watches.

This stingy multimillionaire passed away a few years ago. When this unhappy rich man left the world for good, did he manage to take with him his furniture and buildings, including his precious stocks and shares and money? Was his demise in any way a loss for the poor and hungry homeless refugees who have flocked to Bern?

What do you think of the remark of C.G. Jung who said that the old person who cannot detach himself from life is as weak and mentally diseased as the young person who is incapable of building up his life for himself?

I think that the process of building up one's life is not at all easy in the modern world for many reasons, especially because of the problem of overpopulation, the difficulties involved in receiving a good education, the dearth of housing and the lack of sufficient jobs. Is there anything in the whole process of living that is not a problem today? In my younger days I realised that life was going to be a struggle. Several decades have passed now and it must be said that life is an even greater struggle than what it used to be.

We are technologically advancing at a tremendous pace, we have more gadgets and travelling is easier and faster, but has the quality of life increased? Amidst all this outward prosperity, have the young people found emotional and personal fulfilment? Are they not as complicated and frustrated and unhappy as their counterparts of previous times?

Without a good knowledge of how computers operate one is ill-equipped for most jobs now a days. Jung belonged to a period during which computers were not used, whereas the young persons of the contemporary world are obliged to be computer-literate. They have to acquire this new skill, and if some of them discover that they cannot somehow rise to this new challenge, can we rightly blame them for their inability? If Jung were still alive, I am sure that he would have outshone his contemporaries.

Without the use of a computer, Jung succeeded in acquiring much knowledge; like Erasmus and Darwin, Jung's seminal works are part of the cultural heritage of mankind. Today, however, with the assistance of a computer, one can become extremely erudite, yet how many are keen on delving deeply into any subject? Are there any great thinkers in the world? What I notice everywhere is that most people, on account of the fact that they are computer-literate, put on scholarly airs. With the help of computers many persons acquire a smattering of a subject and then talk and behave as though they are experts in that field! Because of the computer we can amass information, but do we necessarily become wise? In ancient times people knew less but they thought more; today we know a lot but rarely think profoundly. Jung immersed himself in reading, but the present generation of young people are telling me that, because of the existence of the computer, books have all become redundant!

Is the plight of the young the same as the plight of the old who cannot detach themselves from life? I think that both the young and the old are finding their respective situations problematical. It is difficult to say which category — the young or the old — has a heavier burden to carry.

It is necessary to ask a fundamental question. Since the young are required to grow very attached to life, and then detach themselves from it when they are old, would it not be far better if they could remain detached from life from the very beginning? For example, if a young person never develops any attachment to money, power, fame, glory or sex, will not that individual be able to live like a sage throughout life?

The young have to be introduced to a completely new set of values wherein there is an emphasis on Gandhian simplicity, austerity and indifference to riches. We must frown upon the accumulation of wealth. We must tell them that it is far better to have a compassionate heart than to have a big bank balance.

What do you think of Jung's statement that it would be good if we could view death as only a transition, as part of an unknown great long process of life?

I am glad to know that Jung has explained this matter so clearly.

The teaching relating to samsara is an essential part of the Indian religious tradition. According to Hindu, Jain and Buddhist thought, we have all become entangled in this seemingly ceaseless process of births and deaths, which is called samsara. We live our miserable lives and pass away, only to be reborn and die again, followed by another life and yet another life, apparently *ad infinitum,* until there is a sudden ending to this long and sorrowful series of lives. That rare event happens when there is spiritual Illumination.

The Hindus maintain that all these successive lives are experienced by a so-called soul, which they believe exists eternally, whereas Buddhists simply say that what gets reborn is not the soul, which is nothing but a mere mental invention. What gets reborn is not the imaginary soul, but the psychological tendencies, dispositions and cravings. If a person succeeds in dissolving and thereby totally eliminating these tendencies, dispositions and cravings, then there will be nothing left to be reborn. In other words, as there is no longer any residuary karma, the samsaric process ceases once and for all.

We are amazed by the extraordinary talents of infant prodigies. Mozart was able to compose music at an age when many a boy would be learning to speak. Children who are born with such rare abilities are only giving expression to talents that they had laboriously acquired in previous lives. The boy Ramana (later known as Ramana Maharshi), the great sage of India, found spiritual Liberation when he was still a boy, without having to go through a long period of spiritual preparation or sadhana in his final life. Those who are sceptical about rebirth would do well to ponder over this question.

The joys and sorrows that we experience are not always related to, nor are they always traceable to, the thoughts and deeds of our present life. Often it is the case that we are simply reaping what we had sown in a previous life of which we have no remembrance. When children are born physically or mentally handicapped, we naturally feel sorry for them. Our hearts go out to them and we try to help them. They may not be aware of the fact that they, too, are paying off past debts in the sense that they are suffering the consequences of their malicious intentions and misdeeds of their bygone lives.

Theists blame God, the Creator created by their clever minds, for all their misfortunes. What they fail to understand is that, if anyone is to blame, it is only they themselves.
As Shakespeare so wisely observed:

> *"Men at some time are masters of their fates:*
> *The fault, dear Brutus, is not in our stars,*
> *But in ourselves, that we are underlings."*
> (*Julius Caesar* act 1 sc. 2)

The understanding or the realisation that our current life is only a link in a very long chain of lives and deaths results in a great sense of personal responsibility. We know, therefore, that unless we live righteously now, we will have to accept the results of our thoughts, and the deeds that follow therefrom, either in this very life or in subsequent ones.

How many have a deep insight into the problem of terminating this cycle of births and deaths? I think the chances of being born in non-human form are far greater than the chance of being born in human form. For example, in our homes and flats the number of human beings in residence are extremely few in comparison to the number of non-humans therein, such as ants and spiders and other visible creatures as well as innumerable non-visible forms of life such as microbes. Human beings are only a minority. It clearly shows that birth in human form does not happen often. In fact, it is very rarely that one is born with a human body. There is unfortunately an insufficient recognition of this truth. But once the truth dawns on us that we are singularly privileged to be having human bodies, we would naturally start doing everything possible to prolong our lives. We would treasure life, taking the right food, never overworking, never depriving the body of long periods of rest and never pouring our energies into useless pursuits. Therefore, not only must we endure the financial and other hardships of life but also learn to live with all our minor and major illnesses. Life is so precious that only the insane would ever want to throw it away. Realising the relative infrequency of our appearance as human beings in this cycle, how many are able to see the importance and the urgency of putting our inner houses in order right now, in this very life? This indeed is the supreme purpose of life.

Now, my question: What kind of responsibility towards life do you feel, in view of the fact that the old person (also because of health reasons) can only cut back on his activities as death approaches?

How true! As Yogaswami, the celebrated saint of Sri Lanka, used to say, "The time is short but the subject is vast." We must certainly stop those of our activities that are useless. Life should never be allowed to degenerate into a series of incessant activities, for every minute of life is very precious. Every human being, regardless of age, must have this sense of urgency.

No one is going to live forever. Even a little child can die at any moment. When death comes, it arrives suddenly without giving us months or weeks of advance warning. One can be young and healthy in body, but even so the possibility of death is always there. The insecure nature of life is such that every human being is always in imminent danger of death. As one grows older and older, and as the curtain of life is about to be drawn, one becomes painfully conscious that death is impatiently waiting just round the corner. If only death would get frightened and run away!

Because of the afflictions of old age, one must give special attention to the body. The bones become brittle, one gets easily tired and irritable. The young should recognise these special difficulties; the old, on the other hand, must not burden the young with an endless catalogue of their complaints. The young can at least give the old an affectionate hearing. There is a nice saying that a problem shared is a problem halved.

As the body ages it requires light exercises, not strenuous ones. Simple hatha yoga postures are especially excellent for the elderly. It is immensely beneficial to spend much time in the open air, getting away from all the pollution and deadly petroleum fumes of the city. It is best to minimise one's visits to the centres of towns and cities and thereby avoid the terrible traffic noises that unavoidably strain the nerves. In order to regenerate the body, it is absolutely necessary to inhale oxygen, which naturally takes place when walking in wide-open spaces such as forests, parks and beaches. Simply sitting quietly under a tree, inhaling the precious gift of the tree, which is oxygen, can be sheer bliss. We must not forget to thank the tree for all the shade it gives. Beautiful trees are such a joy to behold. They look even more lovely when *Devas* or invisible celestial beings take up residence in them.

The constant renewal of the mind is as important as the constant regeneration of the body. For instance, if we fail to let go the dead past, if we do not throw away the long accumulated cravings and bitter resentments, not excluding our minor resentments, then all these, like deeply disturbed ghosts, will always haunt and trouble the psyche not only in the remaining years of this life but also in the lives to come.

As I grow older I feel increasingly responsible for myself. This feeling gathers strength because of the realisation that one is socially isolated. The vast majority have a certain negative attitude towards the aged, viewing them suspiciously as though the aged were alien visitors from another planet who must be compelled to leave soon, thereby enabling the younger members of society to live freely without any interference from the old in their lives. The young also see the old as a nuisance .The young resent the criticisms that are levelled at them. When an elderly person dies, I can often read the thoughts of the deceased's younger relatives who feel relieved, often thinking and saying to themselves, "Good bye and good riddance!" Such is the heartlessness of the younger generation. Exceptionally, the young weep when their kith and kin pass away. For these reasons there is this fear that in old age one will always have to fend for oneself. Although it is good to devote some time to charitable work and help the world, still I feel that, except for a few loved ones such as one's wife, none will help if there is a crisis such as an accident or an illness.

Do the old have a moral responsibility to be of assistance to the economically, socially, educationally and emotionally deprived? I can certainly help poor persons by giving them some food, clothes, medicines and books. I can also console them when they are depressed and unhappy, yet I realise more than ever before that I cannot help others in a fundamental way. I can neither change their character nor their inner nature. It is, in a sense, rather foolish to start worrying about the sad state of the world. In this sense I cannot personally change the world but I can, at least, try to change myself inwardly.

When I was a teenager I used to be very friendly with several adults who were considerably older than me. The age difference was never a barrier to friendships. Most of my close friends were aged, and one of them was an invalid. He was a permanently paralysed Parsee gentleman in his seventies or eighties. As he lived next door to my home in Colombo, it was my practice to visit him often. He was quite fond of me. What long and fascinating conversations we used to have! Poor Mr Rustomjee hardly had any visitors. This tall and dignified man, always dressed in white pyjamas and a long white shirt extending to his knees, spent his days reading newspapers. His black cap was in sharp contrast with his fair complexion. Only his special servant and his three sons (two leading lawyers and an eminent surgeon) looked after him. All the neighbours avoided him like the plague. They did not know what they were missing by not paying him visits. They did not know what a great joy it was to hear him reminiscing about the good old days of his childhood in Bombay and his later life as a merchant in Colombo.

Quite early in life I learned a lot from Mr Rustomjee, especially about the dual principles of good and evil or light and darkness that characterise the Parsees' very ancient religious system of Zarathustra. The moment the street lights were switched on in the late evenings, he would say, "Excuse me for a moment," lifting his arm above his head as a gesture of adoration. This was the only arm that he was able to move for the other one was paralysed. Light for him was symbolic of the Highest. The mere sight of a light or fire had for him a great spiritual significance. Then he would proceed to say a Zoroastrian prayer. He would always feel a deep sense of revulsion against the sacrilegious habit of smoking.

I find that the members of the younger generation are aloof and distant. Often in the streets they do not even return my greetings. I am willing to give them information, knowledge and wisdom, not to mention my friendship. They do not seem to be greatly interested in anything in particular. They take some interest in fashionable clothes, attractive cars, flashy and terribly noisy motorbikes, exciting sports, the latest computers, having parties frequently and enjoying hallucinogenic drugs. During their short-lived adolescence they begin to take a passionate interest in sex. The addiction to sex, like the addiction to alcohol, can often last for an entire lifetime. Very few free themselves from it. The desire to change society and alter the course of human history does not seem to exist any more. Youthful idealism, alas, seems to be a thing of the past.

I have hardly any communication with the younger generation. There is no rapport between us. Fortunately, I have no children. My nieces and nephews and other relations show a lack of respect for my feelings. They neither answer my letters nor convey their thanks if I should send them gifts. On the whole, they have a high self-esteem. I find them rather rude to their elders and extremely self-centred. The young behave as though they alone are the owners of the entire world. If I may make another generalisation, the young seem to see the old as a lot of useless garbage that should be soon discarded. However, I do not hate them for what they think and do.

I continue leading my reclusive life, not just because the young people's unfriendliness borders on hostility, but almost entirely because it is so peaceful and pleasant to distance oneself from society. I am happy. My inner life is rich and full of treasures that is known only to a few.

Dear Gerda, I have tried very hard to answer your questions. My answers are not infallible. In a few years' time, if these questions were posed again, I would probably answer them differently.

When writing this essay I have borne in mind the fact that what we have discussed are issues that every human being will have to face sooner or later, especially if he or she lives long enough. People are living longer now than they used to do and this tendency will probably increase in the future. The generations to come might not have the same curiosity as that of times past. Life is becoming rather superficial and the older people may not want to ask these fundamental questions that you have raised. The unborn generations will probably have more wealth and enjoy more leisure, but in comparison with the generations of the past, they might not necessarily have deeper insights into life.

Yours affectionately,
Susunaga.

"The man of little learning ages like an ox,
His muscles grow but not his wisdom."
— Dhammapada, 152

A lay benefactress of the Buddha by the name of Visakha once visited him. She was accompanied by a group of women who, unknown to Visakha, were all drunk. They started singing and dancing in the presence of the Master. Then the Buddha made a statement:

"While this world is always burning,
Why is there laughter? Why is there joy?
You who are in darkness,
Why do you not look for a light?"
— Dhammapada, 146

The world is always burning in the sense that it is in a constant state of change. The body is changing. It is subject to old age, decay and death. Living in the world entails a lot of suffering. We try to escape from suffering by means of short spells of so-called pleasures and a thousand diversions. In yet another sense the world is always burning — we burn with anger and numerous desires. There are the flames of fear, jealousy, hatred, passion and vengeance. Our violence flares up again and again. By the light of the Dharma we can, if we only try, dispel the prevailing darkness.

7

Why Suffer from Depression ?

Dear Catherine

It is my intention to address myself to the specific problem posed in your letter.

You have stated that "I am struggling with manic depression. I have just started taking Lithium and will soon begin talk therapy as well, yet I am far from optimistic that I will ever be free of this debilitating illness. For this reason, I am approaching you for advice. Are there any particular prayers, meditations, or other treatments, such as homeopathy, which you personally could recommend in order to come out from under this dark cloud which hangs over me? I feel desperate for a solution, and while I know that this isn't exactly your field, I consider you a learned man of great wisdom, and would like your opinion."

It is a well-known fact that even wise and learned persons are prone to depression!

On those rare occasions when I feel very unhappy and lack any enthusiasm for anything, I know how to handle it, and the depression disappears before long.

I am only a Doctor of Letters — not a medical practitioner: it would be presumptuous and dangerous to treat you medically.

At the outset I wish to dispel the fairly widespread belief that there is a permanent and satisfactory pharmaceutical remedy. There are numerous medicines, pills and drugs for sale but do any of them provide a lasting solution? Is there a medical remedy that can prevent the recurrence of the condition?

Over the years I have successfully helped several friends to deal with this difficulty. I did so without resorting to drugs, medicines or pills.

Strictly speaking, depression is not an illness but a passing psychological state of being in low spirits or feeling blue. But by regarding it as an 'illness', or 'disease', it is often the case that the poor patient becomes even more depressed! So the first requirement is a radical change of attitude to what is called 'depression'.

This morning I woke to a terrible day. It was cold and rainy. The skies were all grey. What a depressing sight! For here in the Provence, which is rightly famous for her deep blue skies and bright sunshine, one usually awakens to the sound of birds singing. I was in low spirits for about two minutes but that emotion quickly disappeared the moment I realised that such weather is only natural in the autumn as the northern hemisphere is now further away from the sun. Seeing that simple truth enabled the mind to disentangle itself from depression. Facing reality is the factor that liberates the mind. This point needs emphasising because I often noticed in depressed people a certain ingrained reluctance to see things as they truly are.

There is the world of reality and the world of illusion. The term 'world of reality' refers to the gloomy actualities of everyday life — facing facts, seeing things exactly as they exist, and especially the non-avoidance of what is ugly, painful or unpleasant. In contrast, the term 'world of illusion' means the tendency to prefer *what should be* to *what is*; it is the unfortunate habit of holding onto memories that are pleasant instead of dropping them; it also refers to living in a fantasy world.

Many persons suffer from depression when their hair starts greying. They are horrified when they suddenly discover that they are no longer young. They start dyeing their hair. I have had no difficulty whatsoever accepting the fact that my hair is grey. What is the point of being pathologically concerned about my appearance? I do not want to look like a young man, as I am no longer one. Since I prefer the world of reality to the world of illusion I do not get depressed.

Depression is a form of unhappiness, especially when it persists for a long time. In this connection I must refer to that famous playwright and writer — 'GBS' as he was known throughout the world. Once George Bernard Shaw was filmed giving an interview. He was requested to give his recipe for happiness. Shaw immediately replied that if one were very active all one's life, there would never be a free moment when one would ask the question, 'Am I happy or unhappy?' When a man immerses himself in his work, hobbies, politics, social welfare programmes, reading, writing, sport or any activity whatsoever for that matter, it is certainly possible for him to *escape* from depression. But then his life will be nothing more than a constant search for escapes. Escapes are only short-term palliatives that do not solve the cause of the difficulty called depression. Escapes temporarily reduce distress without actually curing the cause of depression. The vast majority, I find, are easily satisfied with palliatives for which there is a tremendous market! But those who do not have such a superficial outlook on life would much rather directly confront depression and thereby discover its cause. We shall discuss this question in due course.

What nearly every depressed person lacks is *joie de vivre* or a feeling of great joy or happiness. They no longer enjoy life. In their eyes life has become nothing more than a terribly boring series of actions or duties that have to be performed. In extreme cases this absence of enthusiasm for living results in their viewing life as a horrible ordeal. Even simple daily routines, such as getting out of bed, performing one's ablutions, having a shower and dressing oneself, are seen as daunting tasks, hence their lives move slowly. Therefore in offices and factories depressed workers tend to be considerably slower than their co-workers. Whenever there is a period of retrenchment in the economy these unfortunate depressed workers, on account of their slowness compounded by their low self-esteem, are usually among the first employees to get the sack. So in their own interest depressed persons must get rid of their disorder.

In Colombo, I used to know a very interesting English theosophist called Peter Harper who spent much of his life in Sri Lanka and

Malaysia. Whenever any of Harper's employees suffered from depression, he would strongly advise against eating any food. He said, "a fast lasting twenty-four hours, or several days if necessary, will pep you up. When you're feeling down you should avoid food. Please understand that the temporary absence of the mysterious life force, which is normally within you, caused your depression. But once your starving stomach starts growling with hunger, you will find that the life force suddenly returns. All of a sudden there will be a great zest for life. Then you will start working with a certain elan."

During the decade spent in Australia I met many depressed people. My overall impression is that far more women than men are afflicted with this condition but I may be mistaken. Whoever is a worrier runs the risk of becoming mentally depressed. Once an Australian colleague was feeling very depressed. Holding his hand, I said, "Cheer up, cheer up. Life is too short to be burdened with silly personal problems! What do you do when you are feeling tired after a game of tennis? You take a rest, don't you? Then you recover from your tiredness. Similarly, when your mind is tired, what you need is a rest. Take a rest!"

He listened to me carefully. No sooner had he followed my advice than the fellow was back to normal. The moral is that whenever there is an onset of depression it is better to be alone so that one has the opportunity not only to relax and recover quietly but also to reflect on the important psychological factors in the crisis.

A young and innocent-looking woman by the name of Geraldine was my typist when I served as a librarian in the Parliament of South Australia. Hers was a single-parent family. Single-handedly she tried to raise her little son. She had grown extremely fond of the boy. She not only felt very let-down by her partner's desertion but was also locked in an acrimonious dispute over the custody of the child. Custody was awarded to the child's father on the grounds that Geraldine was a drug-addict. The subsequent separation from her beloved son resulted in Geraldine suffering from manic depression. Never did she recover from the parting. It was a terrible blow.

A few times Geraldine attempted suicide. After one such attempt I got into a long conversation with this distraught woman. On that occasion I said, "Oh, Geraldine! Why do you say that the afterlife would be happier for you? Come off it! We don't really know what the afterlife holds in store for us, do we? It might be paradise. It might be bloody hell. One can never be sure about it. So don't be dissatisfied with your lot. Life on planet Earth isn't that bad after all. In a world with millions of homeless refugees, you at least have a roof above your head. In an overpopulated world in which the vast majority rarely enjoy a square meal, you at least have plenty of food and drink. As regards the custody of your child, you haven't actually lost him. He is alive and well. He lives in another part of Australia where he will grow up happily. Someday you will surely meet him again. Aren't you a lucky mum? Geraldine, don't take your life! Don't kill yourself, I beg you! Those who kill themselves and thereby experience an agonising death might be reborn as hungry and restless ghosts. Do think about these things and don't behave stupidly!"

All my heartfelt words did not come to anything. She was absent from work for a few days. Then one morning the staff of Parliament House in Adelaide received the devastating news that Geraldine had suddenly died the previous night following an overdose of heroin.

One of the interesting characters I met in Adelaide was a woman in her thirties who told me that out of the sheer goodness of her pure heart she spent all her time taking care of those helpless men and women who were the victims of chronic depression. Somewhat surprised, I asked Jill (not her real name) a few questions.

"Is that all you do? Tell me, what do you do for a living?"

"Sir, I suppose you have to work,' she remarked, smiling in a superior manner, "because I don't have to — you see, I'm quite rich now, although I was penniless when I first came to Australia."

Jill provided me with a detailed description of the various selfless services that she was rendering to the depressed.

"There are literally thousands of depressed folk in this city but they are somehow reluctant to admit that they are desperately lonely and much in need of human company. In my list I always have about 50 depressed people whom I regularly meet every few days."

"Do they like you?"

"Yes,' replied Jill with an enthusiastic smile, "because they thoroughly enjoy my company. I'm the only one who gives them flowers. I'm the only friend who kisses them on both cheeks and gives them big hugs. They feel loved. They are painfully aware that they have to live in a loveless world. I crack jokes and their sad faces brighten up. I take them out to restaurants on their birthdays. We go for drives through the Adelaide hills. When it's very hot we sunbathe together on the beach. We hold hands and walk great distances together. Once a month depressed persons have the pleasure of accompanying me when we go to local concerts. There is something else that I do which is important. I make them talk. They love to talk, as ours is a world in which hardly anyone has time to listen to another's personal complaints. During our long chats I draw out from them all their hidden worries. After every conversation they feel extremely well. Their silly depressions are no more! Many of them are so old that they lack friends or relations. I play the role of friend and relation. Between us there is a very strong emotional bond."

"And when they die," I asked, 'don't you feel sad?"

"Why should I feel sad?" she remarked casually, "I'm never sad but happy. It always gives me a thrill when I discover that in their wills I'm the sole heir to their fortunes."

Australia is truly the land of opportunity! The less said about wealthy Jill the better. The moral of this account is that society must beware of those who are hell-bent on exploiting the plight of the depressed to gain financial and other advantages.

In my experience, a sense of physical well-being is helpful to keep my short-lived low spirits at bay. A good night's sleep of eight hours and a twenty-minute siesta after lunch is a *sine qua non* for the regeneration of the body; thirty minutes of hatha yoga every day keeps the body supple and retards the ageing process; a healthy vegetarian diet is not only nutritionally superior to all other foods but also ensures peace within oneself because of the awareness that one is not a party to the killing of animals; rising early at the crack of dawn and seeing the sunrise and the crimson skies is an exhilarating experience; having a quick cold shower each morning and doing breathing exercises in the fresh open-air not only improves the circulation but also oxygenates the system; solitary walks in the woods provide opportunities to commune with nature; growing flowers, plants and organic vegetables in your garden is excellent for relaxation; keep the usage of your car (assuming that you really need one) to an absolute minimum and go for long walks instead, thus activating the muscular system; never destroy the delicate sensitivity of the organism by polluting it with alcohol, tobacco and dangerous drugs. The interrelationship between body and mind is amazingly close. When the body is healthy, sensitive and vibrant, it will not fail to make a beneficial impact on the mind, and consequently curtail the tendency towards depression.

A writer who is prone to depression told me that some of his best books were written when he was feeling low. "Depression is a tonic," he observed, "it is a forceful spur to write well. I can't write if I'm feeling proud or if there is self-satisfaction. Creativity flows from the depths of despair."

When I first heard Beethoven's music it suddenly struck me that the inward state of the great composer was anything but calm, peaceful and happy. The erratic movements in his music stand out clearly. It is a feature that has not diminished in any way the quality of Beethoven's works. Many great musicians, artists and writers have suffered from severe depression. It is not clear whether or not their achievements were the outcome of their depression. It is significant though that depression was not an impediment to creativity.

In this connection I must mention the case of a professor whom I used to know. He managed to keep his depression well under control, never allowing it to get the better of him by uninterruptedly listening to the soothing and inspiring music of Mozart. In his study Mozart tapes would be played all the time, even when he was reading, writing, researching or simply thinking with his eyes closed.

While the professor's fondness for Mozart was certainly in good taste, he need not have resorted to this escape, nor to any other escape for that matter, had he taken the trouble to discover for himself the underlying causes of his depression, and thereby eliminate the disorder once and for all. In addition to reading many books, the learned man could well have done his homework by reading the most important book of all, which is the book of himself. This unprinted 'book' is about the exploration of the inner world of the psyche. We shall be discussing this question of meditation and self-knowledge at the end.

In recent years I have been closely associated with two manic-depressives. Both of them are friends. Their coldness and distance has resulted in a superficial friendliness on their part. The flower of friendship has never really blossomed as they keep themselves aloof from me. Although they never reciprocate the kindness that I have at all times unfailingly shown to them, the warmth of my friendship with them has never abated. For the reason that they are obsessionally attached only to themselves, rarely do they take an interest in the welfare and happiness of others. Occasionally they try to do selfless deeds but on the whole they are self-centred. They wallow in self-pity. They are full of self-doubt and they lack self-confidence. This is only an incomplete description of them.

I first met Annienella (not her real name) on Thursday market day. A tiny bespectacled old lady, she was standing outside the post office and crying her eyes out.

"What's troubling you?"

"Hypertension! Death is around the corner!" she complained tearfully.

Realising that Annienella was making a great public show of her so-called suffering in order to become the centre of attention, I immediately gave her some grapes. She suddenly smiled and her depression was in abeyance.

Central to Annienella's condition is an intense and irrational sense of loss and the fear that she lacks the capacity to survive her self-centred emotional crises. This sense of loss is sometimes real but often it exists only in her fertile imagination (I should mention that the lady is an accomplished linguist and an excellent teacher of Spanish and Italian). Religious and conscientious, Annienella always criticises herself by saying "I've forgotten to do this", "I should have done that", "I wasn't careful enough" and "I should have foreseen this problem". She is always conscience-stricken.

Annienella is full of self-criticism. Once she was weeping that the prices of fruits and vegetables in France were much higher than those in her native Italy.

"I should have done all my shopping in Genoa," she would say with much sadness.

"Stop grumbling," I said, "and pull yourself together! Are you facing starvation? You are a rich woman with properties in France and Italy! Why worry about high prices?"

That comment helped her to calm herself down, especially because it reminded her not to be out of touch with reality. She was prone to making herself miserable and depressed by believing that she was poverty-stricken. This terrible feeling of insecurity was a hangover from her younger days in Italy when her family were not well-to-do. Her past was haunting her. She became the prisoner of her unpleasant memories.

One day Annienella was weeping because her husband's daughter by a previous marriage was on the verge of total blindness. The daughter was a chronic diabetic patient. It took a long time to convince her that she was not personally responsible for the illness. Annienella was feeling guilty and full of remorse that she had personally done little or nothing to prevent the blindness. She had to be reminded that she had over the years tended her daughter with loving care. The blindness, I remarked, was caused by the daughter's bad karma in her present life or in a previous one. That explanation helped to calm Annienella down but only temporarily.

The trouble with Thomas (not his real name) is that he is always full of harsh fault-finding of himself. He likes flagellating himself. He does not beat his body of course, but he, so to speak, enjoys beating his mind mercilessly. I have associated with this manic-depressive for over thirty years, which is a long period. Most of the time he is so depressed that getting out of bed is quite a struggle. Much time is spent in bed. Seldom does he answer letters. An emotionally disturbed man, Thomas loses his temper with friends who give him presents. He feels that he does not deserve gifts because of his moral degeneration. He eats frugally and feels guilty every time he is given a sumptuous meal.

Thomas was an ardent communist in his student days. His country in which he continues to live is a mixed economy. Thomas holds himself personally responsible for the fact that a socialist revolution never took place there! He thinks that he has only himself to blame for the problems of poverty, unemployment, crime and corruption in the land of his birth! His hatred of society is directed against himself. Although he regularly reads the daily newspapers, Thomas has very little interest in the world outside himself. The pathologically melancholic world in which he dwells begins and ends with himself. He is almost incapable of love or affection for anyone. His efforts to feign affection are motivated by the desire to ensure that others take an active interest in him.

Ours is a dark age in which sexual promiscuity has become more the norm rather than the exception. Not surprisingly, Thomas is inextricably addicted to sex. At first his sexuality found expression in masturbation; later in his youth he preferred homosexual acts to any other form of carnal indulgence; in his adult life he changed over to heterosexual acts; now in his old age he has reverted to masturbation or autoeroticism. After every sexual act of whatever form, Thomas experiences not only a considerable depletion of energy but also manic depression. He has a guilty conscience following every sexual act. He worries himself sick and feels thoroughly miserable. Then he asks me to put him out of his misery as though I were capable of waving a magic wand and making him happy instantaneously.

My advice to Thomas has always been as follows: "Sex is neither sinful nor non-sinful. But since the purpose of sex is procreation, not recreation, it would be better if you can try and abstain from sex altogether and lead a pure life."

Then he would protest, "You are attempting to take away the last remaining pleasure in life."

Next I would explain, "You are trying to escape from manic

depression by means of sex. That is what you have been doing for years. But the day you free yourself from manic depression you will find that you are no longer enslaved by sex."

All my concerned advice fell on deaf ears and the man stopped writing to me.

Hippocrates, the father of medicine, used the word 'melancholia' to describe depression. Sigmund Freud's *Mourning and Melancholia* is a seminal work on the subject.

Can psychotherapists and psychoanalysts really help you? They are all capable of assisting superficially but not profoundly. They touch the periphery of the problem and not its centre. Their approach is fundamentally flawed because they insist on using the mind without first of all unconditioning it. As the mind is our only instrument of inquiry, its purification via meditation is a *sine qua non* of investigation. What is the point of investigating with a distorted and conditioned mind, since everything we perceive will inevitably be distorted? To understand the mind one must never turn outwards. By never regarding the mind as an external object for investigation, but by turning inwards it is possible to understand the nature of the mind and its manifold tendencies. This subjective approach to the mind automatically takes place when one starts meditating.

The onset of any form of depression is a sign that the inner house is in a state of disorder. Meditation is the best means of bringing about order and sanity. Every human being has the innate capacity to put his or her house in order. Do not permit anyone to cash in on your condition.

If you turn inside your own mind, the mind gets turned inside out, revealing all that is hidden and hitherto unknown. The memories of a thousand yesterdays, including the unresolved problems and your personal traits going back as far as your previous lives, will begin to surface. You can do this yourself without seeking the assistance of anyone.

"*You are your own saviour,*" taught the Buddha.

It seems to me that meditation is the only solution to manic depression.

There are two forms of meditation — Occidental Meditation and Oriental Meditation. We shall consider both types of meditation, which nicely complement each other. Occidental Meditation consists in ruminating over certain stimulating questions. Oriental Meditation consists in self-observation; it is the path of self-knowledge.

Occidental Meditation

Distressing traumas do result in manic depression. It is possible that you have forgotten or suppressed them. So long as they remain dormant, these traumas will adversely affect your mental health. Just to jog your memory, please permit me to pose several questions:

> Is there in you a lifetime of pent-up anger?
> Within you is there a boiling sense of the injustices of life?
> Are you a victim of parental neglect?
> Is your present suffering caused by not having had the basic necessities because of war or natural catastrophes?
> Did you ever suffer in silence when those who were near and dear to you failed to show any affection?
> Have years of unhappiness or poverty, if such was the case, left their mark in your mind?
> Have you had a love-hate relationship with anyone?
> If you have ever been jilted, does it still upset you?
> Are you really happy in your present country of residence?
> Concerning your decision to marry a foreigner, was it met with the approval of your parents, relations and friends?
> Do you have any other psychological scars?

Oriental Meditation

As I have examined this subject in depth in a recently published book of mine titled, *Nirvana: the Highest Happiness* (Delhi: New Age Books), please permit me to include an excerpt therefrom:

The constant undistorted observation of oneself results in the exposure of the hidden depths of the unconscious. Such observation or awareness is that pure flame which alone will burn away all our psychological complications. While it is comparatively easy to observe one's thoughts and feelings superficially, it is far more difficult to be aware of the hidden forces underlying these thoughts and feelings — the unknown fears, hopes, ambitions and urges that shape our day-to-day behaviour. Meditation then is the golden means whereby the conditioned mind becomes unconditioned. A life that is not dedicated to meditation soon becomes superficial, miserable and dull; on the other hand, the person who cares to meditate becomes psychologically cleansed. Only in this state of inner purity, declared the Buddha, does one experience the bliss of Liberation.

> *"This, monks, is Nanda's mindfulness*
> *And clear comprehension.*
> *Here, monks, for Nanda*
> ***Feelings** are understood as they arise,*
> *As they remain present,*
> *As they pass away;*
> ***Perceptions** are understood as they arise,*
> *As they remain present,*
> *As they pass away;*
> ***Thoughts** are understood as they arise,*
> *As they remain present,*
> *As they pass away.*
> *This, monks, is Nanda's mindfulness*
> *And clear comprehension."*
>
> — Anguttara Nikaya viii, 9

Mindfulness consists in the immediate understanding of feelings, perceptions and thoughts as and when these arise. It is not that one understands them later, retrospectively, through a process of recollection, with closed eyes and seated cross-legged, which is the traditionally accepted posture for meditation.

One can, of course, recall feelings, perceptions and thoughts long after their occurrence. But, evidently the Buddha has recommended the awareness of feelings, perceptions and thoughts right here and now.

Awareness takes place only in the present, from moment to moment; it is seeing ourselves with detachment all the time; this is the simple and impartial observation of all aspects of ourselves all the time; it is watching the current in action, as it happens, as opposed to watching or examining it later, which would be like carrying out a post mortem of feelings, perceptions and thoughts long after they have passed away.

Of all the books in existence, the most important one is the book of self-knowledge. The really ignorant are not the illiterate folk but those who never read this marvellous book. This tome has never been published. Even if you were to live to a ripe old age and acquire a reputation for your remarkable achievements, your life would still have been lived in vain, if you have failed or forgotten to read this book. 'Reading the book' and 'meditating' are one and the same.

Allowing your thoughts and emotions to present themselves fully and unimpededly — and watching them at the same time non-judgementally — is far better than bottling them up, which is often the cause of depression. By the powerful searchlight of awareness one can clearly see all one's anxieties, fears, frustrations and jealousies as well as everything that is negative and troublesome. Thus you can cleanse yourself and prevent the recurrence of depression.

In the same way that you observe the flow of heavy traffic on a highway, can you not watch the seemingly endless procession of thoughts and feelings? This you can do all the time, regardless of whether or not you are calm. When you are engaged in any activity, be it eating, drinking, exercising, reading, bathing or walking, can you not simply watch yourself as you do these things, neither approving nor disapproving of what you see within yourself? Do not interfere with your reactions. Do not say "this is a good thought" or "this is a bad thought". Do not make any comment whatsoever about any thought or feeling. All you have to do is to observe impartially everything that is taking place within you. Just look at yourself without taking sides! Look at the activities of the inner stream from the vantage point of inactivity! In other words, look at action within from the state of inaction!

As you observe your thought process you might see in a flash the faces of various persons who in the past caused you much pain or much joy. It might be the face of a teacher who unfairly punished you in school, the face of a schoolmate who hated you because you were seen as a rival, the face of a shopkeeper who cheated you and deprived you of money, or even the face of a jealous brother or sister. Now, as you see these faces, take note of your feelings of resentment towards them, but do not tell yourself "how awful! I shouldn't harbour such grudges", or "I must rid myself of such ill will". Never condemn your thoughts or feelings. Never be critical of your thoughts or feelings. *All you have to do is simply to observe them in a neutral way, and then let go of them.* Then you would be purging the mind of its impurities.

The very recognition of the existence of those thoughts and feelings will automatically result in their dissolution. It is the honest acceptance of *the truth of what you actually are*, or the innocent and undistorted observation of yourself *exactly as you are*, that will liberate you from this bothersome burden of resentments. Otherwise, your psychological luggage, so to speak, will cripple your mind and pervert your pure perception as well as leave you embittered for a lifetime.

In the above-mentioned manner, you can also observe your reactions when, for example, someone flatters you, or pays you a compliment by saying "what a pretty face!" or "what a sweet girl!" Observe how your ego expands when there is praise; observe how the ego gets hurt when there is blame. When pride and vanity have also been discarded you will become an inwardly transformed human being who is clear-sighted.

Meditation is not a self-inflicted torture or a punishment; those who are always in a meditative state realise that meditation is actually the joyous experiencing of constant self-discovery and self-rediscovery.

Dear Catherine, in this long letter I have requested you to get involved in meditation. I have no doubt that diligent meditation will help you to overcome manic depression. Meditation is not merely a therapy, but it is also the path to Enlightenment.

Yours sincerely,
Susunaga.

"Now you are like a withered leaf,
The messengers of death are at your side.
Though you are about to depart,
You have no provisions for the journey."
— Dhammapada, 235

"Make yourself an island,
Work hard,
Be wise.
Purged of impurities
And free from craving,
You will reach
The abode of the Ariyas."
— Dhammapada, 236

"The abode of the Ariyas' refers to Suddhavasa or the Pure Abode, wherein live the Anagamins or Non-Returners."

8

Crossing the Stream of Thought

Many indeed are the obstacles in our spiritual path. Going beyond the stream of thought is probably the most challenging problem. The seeker cannot avoid it. Meditation has long been seen as the most effective means of solving the problem. What then is right meditation? A Chinese lady who is interested in Buddhism asked several questions about meditation. I have tried to summarise the salient points of our conversation.

I do not know how to meditate but I'm eager to begin. I haven't still found a suitable spiritual master who can teach me meditation. I think that it is dangerous to meditate without proper guidance.

It is not true that one cannot begin meditation without the guidance of a master. That is the first thing to understand.

Nowadays it is becoming fashionable to say that one practises meditation, isn't that so? In spiritual circles it is very respectable to acquire a reputation as a pious person who spends a lot of time in silent meditation. Recognising that secret desire for name and fame is part of meditation. Don't we take pride in our beauty, talents, abilities, learning, wisdom, wealth, achievements, elevated social status, high caste and so forth? Just being aware of the various vast and trivial things in which we take pride in, simply observing the existence of pride in different forms, without brushing it aside, helps to understand the sinister nature of the ego. Pride has rightly been regarded as one of the seven deadly sins in the Christian tradition. One who has pride that is equal even to a single grain of mustard seed, declared Prophet Muhammad, will fail to enter Paradise. In Hindu literature the term *Ahamkara* stands for egotism, haughtiness or conceit, but actually it has a wider meaning — the conception of one's individuality which is the prime cause of samsaric slavery.

Meditation is nothing other than coming to know the contents of consciousness, which consists of thoughts and feelings. Are we fully awake all the time? Are we aware of this inescapable inner world of ours? Most of the time what happens? We do not succeed in observing our thoughts and feelings as the stream of consciousness flows far too fast. The current of consciousness is so swift and intense that we are simply overpowered by it. Thoughts and feelings arise and disappear like flashes of lightening. One does not seem to have time enough to observe carefully the various currents of thoughts and emotions.

Therefore mustn't I control thought so that the process slows down?

If you try to control or subjugate thought in any way you will find that the thought process starts speeding up and the situation gets worse. But if you stop interfering with the stream, then it slows down. I use the word 'stream' as it is an especially suitable one. Aren't our thoughts and feelings like the ceaseless movement of the waters of a rapid stream?

It is important to realise that any interference with the stream results in making it even more active. If you try to put down by force your thoughts and feelings, instead of giving them free rein and observing them at the same time, you would only have dammed up the stream. So sooner or later the dam will burst under the force and weight of the water. The stream of consciousness, in other words, instead of moving slowly and calmly, becomes hyperactive. Therefore, non-interference with the workings of the mind in any manner is the first step in the right direction.

What are the other steps?

We have long been accustomed to correcting ourselves in a judgmental way. For example, it occurs to a customer, who feels that he has been cheated by a shopkeeper, to slap the latter hard across the face, or to stab him in the stomach with a knife. He is so upset that he wants to take revenge on the dishonest shopkeeper by harming him. Then the customer, conscious of his shameful thoughts, tells himself "I shouldn't think such evil thoughts" and attempts thereby to destroy his aggressive and violent tendencies. Rather than facing the fact that he is simmering with resentment, the man suppresses his anger, thus failing to discover a certain seedy side to his character that had hitherto remained hidden. Now, the truly meditative person never tries to stop the emergence of any thought or feeling whatsoever, but seizes every opportunity to unearth all his troublesome traits. He passively watches the stream in action in the sense that he observes himself *uncensoriously*. He never tells himself "Ah, well, this is a good thought" nor "this is a bad thought". Neither does he tell himself "this is a pleasant and desirable feeling" nor "this is an unpleasant and undesirable feeling." Then what takes place? He suddenly finds that the doors and windows of his mind no longer remain closed and bolted. All the active as well as the inactively dormant fears, hates, frustrations, jealousies, prejudices, likes, dislikes and all the other predispositions begin to surface. All the psychological baggage of an entire lifetime, not excluding the long forgotten baggage of our previous lives, gets thrown out. This process goes on and on and the stream automatically purifies itself. The manifold malignancies of the mind manifest themselves and there is a spiritual metamorphosis.

What is the supreme purpose of life? It is surely the cleansing away of our defilements or imperfections. If I may venture a remark, those who close their eyes to this greatest of all goals would only be wasting their precious lives. They fail to realise that birth as a human being is not only difficult but also very rare. As human beings we have the opportunity to understand that a good many of our psychological characteristics, which collectively constitute our 'personalities' or 'egos', can be traced back to our dim and distant past lives. As the mind unburdens itself, thereby gradually drifting into nothingness, it is noteworthy that there will now take place a slower movement in the former turbulent stream. It still flows but in a considerably quieter manner. Probably someday the stream will quieten down altogether. Probably someday the stream will somehow cease to exist. But let us not speculate about that exalted state as we have not gone thus far.

Several friends have advised me that in order to meditate correctly, one should remain in a noiseless room and sit cross-legged on the floor with the eyes fully or partly closed.

What you have described is certainly a relaxed posture as far as the body is concerned. But the watchful ones do not necessarily feel the need to stay in any particular posture. It is the experience of those who are totally devoted to meditation that their self-observation goes on all the time, regardless of whether or not they are seated cross-legged.

Often I forget to watch myself. I see it as a terrible lapse.

Why do you say that? Why regard meditation as a rigorous discipline, when it is really a passive and effortless state wherein there is no 'I' or 'doer' who is doing the meditation? Meditation is a watchful state in which the 'watcher' is totally absent. During meditation it is nothing but pure Intelligence that operates. For the want of a better word, I call it the Unconditioned State in which there is undistorted perception.

Yes, sometimes we are not watchful. Even during such spells of inattention, contradictory though it may seem, buried memories of traumatic experiences as well as trivial and unimportant events in our lives unexpectedly reveal themselves. It shows that one cannot really run away from the stream. It is active throughout the day, and later at night the stream appears again via images. When we are asleep the stream expresses itself through dreams as though it were wanting to scream like a baby in order to get some attention to itself.

Do you notice any significant difference between the one who meditates and the one who doesn't?

The meditative man discovers a bright new dimension to his life. He has a heightened awareness of his inner world. Someday he might transcend the stream but unfortunately that does not happen that often.

Do you subscribe to the belief that Japa or the repetition of God's name purifies the mind?

Japa is the devotional practice of repeating a specially selected sacred syllable, sound or word such as OM or Hare Krishna. Hearing the same sounds over and over again has a certain hypnotic effect. Have you not noticed that the repetition of any sound, even the ticking of a clock or the beat of a piece of music, especially its regular rhythm, results in a sleep-like state? Japa, like good jazz, is gaining popularity as it is an excellent tranquilliser in a world wherein more and more people are under a lot of stress.

Speaking from personal experience, I know that the mere hearing of sweet and sonorous voices chanting Rama nama is like listening to Mozartesque music that is so soothing. Japa is so pleasant that I can listen to it all day and night without getting bored or tired. Participation in Japa chanting sessions was nearly always an exhilarating experience. On such occasions I have gone into short-lived ecstasies. However, I soon realised that during those ecstatic and blissful moments of so-called self-annihilation the ego never really disappeared in toto, but went into hiding, and thereby continued to exist! So clever and cunning is the fox-like nature of the ego that it is almost impossible to track down the 'I'.

There is a supreme Intelligence that is not of the mind, for the mind is only a transient and superimposed structure on that eternal Source. With the light of that Intelligence one can clearly see why and how the ego was born, why we cling to the fictitious ego as though it were our most treasured possession; we can also understand the ego's true nature, the understanding of which, leads to its eventual demise. That faculty of Understanding or Intelligence alone will eradicate the ego once and for all, although many would like to believe that there are cheap, quick and easy tricks and methods of bringing about its destruction.

What in your opinion is the highest meditation?

What happens when the mind is fully relaxed because it is free from all attachments? Then the mind is quiet *naturally*, not made 'quiet' or forced to be 'still' artificially. Then the thought-process moves very slowly, like a conveyor belt in slow motion. One feels unruffled with the result that the mind starts telling its own story, replaying the records of unresolved problems and repressed memories that lurk in the psyche, doing that of its own accord and revealing all its dark secrets that had until then remained unknown by the conscious mind. Thus when the floodgates of the mind have got opened, the gushing waters of self-knowledge flow freely and uncontrollably until the mind has totally unconditioned itself. Then there is a great silence. It is the silence that is born of inner purity. As the purified mind is no longer under any form of pressure, one arrives at a state of effortless calm in which the mind, without any struggle whatsoever, constantly cleanses itself and hence no new karma gets created. This is the highest meditation in which the mind is passive and inactive, yet extraordinarily alive and alert.

"The disciples of Gautama are always alert
With their attention
Focussed on the Buddha
By day and night."

— Dhammapada, 296

"The disciples of Gautama are always alert
With their attention
Focussed on the Dharma
By day and night."

— Dhammapada, 297

"The disciples of Gautama are always alert
With their attention
Focussed on the Sangha
By day and night."

— Dhammapada, 298

"The disciples of Gautama are always alert.
They take delight
In meditation
By day and night."

— Dhammapada, 301

9

The Cycle of Births and Deaths

Following the publication of a book of mine entitled *My Philosophy of Life*, I received a letter from a good old friend by the name of Stanley Jayaweera. A respected writer and intellectual of Sri Lankan origin, Stanley holds a first class honours degree in Philosophy. Prior to his retirement, he was the Sri Lankan Ambassador to Germany. In his letter Stanley posed several challenging questions, which I tried to answer as best as I can. In reply to his letter I wrote as follows:

January 27, 2003
My dear Stanley

Your letter of January 18th is cheering as it shows good old Stanley's mind in full philosophical form. I will quote from your letter:

"In the very first para you have referred to an 'endless cycle of births and deaths'. How do you know? What proof have you personally that there is such an endless cycle of births and deaths? You speak of 'my previous lives' in the very first page. How do you know that you had an earlier birth? Tell me, what were you in your immediately preceding birth?"

You have been intellectually trained to require proof. Isn't this a criterion of your own making? For me the Truth does not have to be proved because it is self-evident. Do I have to prove that the sun shines or that fire burns? Aren't these pretty obvious?

For the vast majority of Buddhists, rebirth is nothing more than a blind belief. However I have discovered that rebirth is a fact. Let me explain.

I must have been about 4 or 5 years old. I could hardly speak. I was still too young to go to school. One day it occurred to me very strongly that I was different from the other kids with whom I used to play. Besides, I also noticed that my likes and dislikes were very different from those of the other children who were living in the same house. Then I knew that I hadn't acquired my particular traits from my surroundings; I knew that I had brought them along from a previous existence. Unfortunately, I have no recollection of that previous existence.

If I were to ask you, "What were you doing on the 27th of January ten years ago?" or "What were you doing on the 27th of January fifteen years ago" you would probably reply, "I don't remember." Just because you cannot recall what had happened then, does it follow that you did not exist either ten or fifteen years ago?

Our inability to recall the details of our past lives does not necessarily mean that our past lives never existed.

According to the Buddhist scriptures, only Arhats have this capacity to remember past lives, but it is a very significant pointer that they rarely used it. The exercise of Siddhis is frowned upon in both the Hindu and Buddhist traditions. Having the supernormal power to remember the minutiae of our former lives is one thing, but exercising that power is quite another.

Moggallana's psychic faculties were so highly developed that he could relate the details of the past lives of others, including those of his own. The Buddha, however, relegated Mogallana to second place; instead he preferred the outlook and lifestyle of Sariputta, his foremost disciple who, instead of wasting his time on occult hobbies, understood very clearly the transitoriness of all things and the fallacy of the 'I'. That understanding alone is enough: every other attainment is only of secondary importance.

Why is it that in Buddhist sculpture throughout the ages, the statue of Sariputta is always placed on the right side of the Buddha, whereas the statue of Moggallana is always on the left of the Master? It is surely an instruction that the path to Illumination is via self-exploration and self-purification, and never via the development of psychic or extra-sensory faculties that are dormant in man.

Is all the information about my previous lives, if I ever succeed in finding it, going to help me in the task of putting my inner house in order? Not knowing the details of our past lives is not such a loss. All we have to know and understand is what we are right now, because our tendencies and characteristics (our Vasanas) have resulted from the distillation of the experiences of innumerable forgotten lives. The past, in other words, is contained in the present.

Very early in life, as already stated, I was well aware of my dispositions or Vasanas. Did these traits spring up from nowhere? Did my character originate in nothingness? Was my nature the handiwork of a Creator, as many a gullible theist would like to believe? Long before I attended Christian schools, years before I was subjected to Christian propaganda, I surprisingly knew the fact that I had carried over my dispositions from all or some previous lives of which I have no recollection.

During the aforementioned very short period of 4 or 5 years I could not have possibly acquired my dispositions from my environment, especially because in those early days I was a solitary child, who occasionally played games with a few kids with whom there was no close rapport. At that time I had very strong likes and dislikes, which were all peculiarly my own and which were certainly not acquired, but were directly traceable to my unrecorded past that is lost in the mists of time. That past of which one is only vaguely aware, which every sensitive child instinctively knows, this gut feeling which to the 'educated mind' appears to be so unscientific and so irrational, this strange emotional awareness of one's real origins, goes well beyond the moment of conception.

It is before 4 a.m. that I have dreams. There is nothing particularly noteworthy about these dreams. The residuary psychological difficulties related to fears, anxieties, hopes, frustrations and the like find expression in these dreams. During these dreaming spells the 'psychological garbage' gets thrown away, thank goodness, and one feels all the better for these dreams.

Although I am by no means an Arhat, I have a general idea of my past lives.

I get up around 4 a.m., next have a wash, read a bit sometimes, and then go back to bed until 7a.m. This is my normal practice. Often during the quiet period between 4 a.m. and 7 a.m. I have extraordinary experiences. I have had out-of-body experiences but this interesting subject is irrelevant to our present discussion.

After 4 a.m., provided I am calm and free of disturbing influences such as worries or problems, there is a semi-trance-like state in which I either meet people or visit places associated with my previous lives. Often I see the same familiar faces and the same familiar places, which are all totally unrelated to my present life. I also re-live the events of past lives such as enjoyable voyages, fine musical concerts, social events like weddings, feasts and funerals. Then there are those long conversations with people whom I have never seen nor met in my present life. It is amazing that I have managed to talk to friends and relations of past lives, using languages that have long been extinct. Even the colourful and weird dresses and manners of the people I see are so different from those of today. In general, the people I see have rather diminutive figures but they are somewhat larger than pygmies.

I have reason to believe that I have been, as it were, resuscitating certain long buried impressions or memories. It is a pity that I cannot identify the exact locations where these events happened, nor do I know when they happened. I am therefore sometimes disappointed that I never seem to re-experience these very ancient events in the exact chronological sequence in which they took place. Not infrequently it is the case that the buried impressions tend to surface in the wrong chronological order, in the sense that a recorded scene of the 18th century would come before one of the medieval periods!

Once I was joking and chatting to my friends in an ancient Indian bazaar. We were all turbaned and many were bearded. Judging by the clothes that people were wearing, it seemed like a scene from the Moghul period of Indian history. After finishing my shopping, I took leave of my friends and started walking home slowly. I lived in the outskirts of the tiny town. It was evening and still quite hot. I was sweating and my long shirt was wet. Just before reaching my home, I noticed that I was passing an enormous glacier and people were getting ready for ice skating! When two or more impressions or memories get mixed up this is the result! Light complexioned persons like Europeans and North Indians feature prominently in these experiences.

When I see these old records, they fill me with nostalgia for my past lives that are all gone forever. Seeing them again in part is like the replaying of excerpts from old family films. Watching them is fun!

I can assure you that what I am describing is not something that I have invented or imagined. I discount that possibility because I have these supernatural experiences only in states when I am not asleep. They happen, as already mentioned, in semi-trance-like states of consciousness. It is difficult to describe this state accurately. I am quite awake but at the same time I am, as it were, out of this world and in a sphere that is certainly not of this world.

If I may digress for a few moments, let me temporarily forget these past lives and turn my attention back to the present life. On those rare occasions when I go on vacation, either visiting India or parts of southern Europe, I suddenly recognise certain streets and houses that I am seeing for the first time in my current life. So when I am in such places I haven't the slightest doubt that I had been there before in the course of a previous life.

Once while having a conversation with Krishnamurti, I told him of an extraordinary happening. In the following excerpt from my book entitled *J. Krishnamurti As I Knew Him* (Delhi: Motilal Banarsidass, 1988), I give Krishnamurti a full description of the strange event:

"*...I recently visited your parental home. I was curiously wanting to see the sacred puja room in which you were born. Some friends kindly took me to your former home in Madanapalle. I was walking ahead of them in this little town. Although I had never even seen a photograph of your home, I unmistakably identified it the moment I saw it. Besides, I knew all the details of the house's interiors even before entering it. The whole house was strangely familiar. In a trance I walked up the stairs and searched for a religious picture in a room. Much to my regret the picture was missing for it had been removed. But the occupant of the* *house confirmed that I had correctly indicated the exact spot on the wall where the picture had once been hanging..."*

Sometimes in my present life I can also recognise men, women and children as well as animals with which I had been closely associated during bygone lives. If I have had pleasant dealings with a man or woman in a previous life, I find that I tend to be favourably disposed towards that person. I must confess that I occasionally dislike some strangers after meeting them for the first time. This attitude, I think, is a hangover from a previous existence when I was cheated, exploited or badly treated by the person in question.

Dear Stanley, you would probably say that nothing that I have written conclusively proves rebirth. I cannot prove its existence logically. I have a gut feeling that rebirth is a fact. It is a very deep conviction and this has nothing to do with the fact that I was born in Sri Lanka with its predominant Buddhist culture. It is a profound realisation that cannot be proved with incontrovertible personal evidence. Rebirth is not a silly belief. Actually there is no need to prove it. The evidence that I have presented may seem flimsy and unconvincing in your eyes, but are you also going to ignore the evidence of the Illumined One whose 550 past lives have been an inspiration for suffering humanity over the centuries? Are you suggesting that the Jataka stories are complete fabrications?

If there is no 'I', then what is it that is going to be reborn? Only a part of 'me' is going to be reborn. For example, if there is a dropping of my resentments in this very life, these vasanas of hate cannot get reborn. Only the remaining vasanas get transferred. This is the truth in the sense that it is an observable fact for it is neither a theory nor a dogma. This is quite a simple thing to understand. and not at all mysterious.

Yours affectionately,

Susunaga.

10

In Praise of Pacifism

Whenever the world is on the brink of war the protests of pacifists are rarely taken seriously. The moral, ethical and religious standpoints are often ignored and even rejected by the vast majority.

We can ponder over the Buddha's famous words:

"Let us live in love
Among those who hate.
Let us live without hate
While others hate."

In the Jetavana monastery several young monks were tidying a building wherein they wanted to stay. Then several elderly monks arrived at the scene and insisted that they alone had the right to stay there on account of their age and seniority. The senior monks argued that they were deserving this respect. But the younger monks refused to agree to their demand. In the ensuing conflict the elderly monks gave the younger ones a severe beating. The latter were in such great pain that they began to cry.

When he was informed of the violent attacks, the Buddha declared that a monk must never hurt another.

"Everyone is afraid
Of the rod of punishment.
Everyone fears death.
Doing as one would be done by,

One should neither kill
Nor cause other persons to kill."
— Dhammapada, 129

"Everyone is afraid
Of the rod of punishment.
Life is dear to everyone.
Doing as one would be done by,
One should neither kill
Nor cause other persons to kill."
— Dhammapada, 130

Two kingdoms were about to wage war for the possession of a certain embankment. Seeing that the kings and their armies were on the verge of fighting, the Buddha intervened and listened to the allegations and counter-allegations of the contending parties. The Buddha asked them whether the disputed embankment had any intrinsic value apart from its usefulness to people. The reply was that the embankment lacked any intrinsic value whatsoever. The Buddha indicated that in battle the men as well as the kings were liable to get killed. He then posed this question,

"Is the blood of men
Of less intrinsic value
Than a mound of earth?"

The kings answered that the lives of the persons involved in the dispute were indeed priceless.

"In that case," asked the Buddha,
'Are you planning to stake
That which is priceless
Against something
Which has no intrinsic value at all?"

The kings soon came to their senses and a peaceful agreement was reached. The Buddha helped those who were blinded by passion to see the folly of their thoughts and deeds. He did this through friendly discussions in which he reasoned simply, coolly, clearly and logically.

In the teachings of the compassionate Buddha there is no place for the concepts of revenge and retaliation. He showed love to his adversaries. A foolish man once abused him. When the man had finished reviling him the Buddha asked,

> *"If a person declined*
> *To accept a gift made to him,*
> *Then to whom would the gift belong?"*

The man answered that the gift would then belong to the person who offered it. Then the Buddha said,

> *"You have denounced me*
> *But I decline to accept your abuse*
> *And request you*
> *To keep it yourself."*

The Buddha likened a wicked man who abuses a virtuous one to a person who looks up and spits at heaven. The spittle does not smear heaven but returns and soils himself. He also likened a slanderer to one who throws dust at another when the wind is blowing in a contrary direction: the dust returns to him who threw it. Whereas the virtuous man remains unhurt, the abuser cannot help suffering for his misdeeds. It is recorded that the abuser in this story went away ashamed of himself but returned later on to the Buddha, though this time it was to take refuge in him and his teachings.

Probably because of his great reputation as a philosopher and sage all manner of persons visited the Buddha and listened to his discourses. Not infrequently he encountered malicious adversaries who derived a perverted satisfaction by reviling and ridiculing him. On such occasions, as always, he acted with composure and dignity. Without losing his temper in even the most trying situations, he often took pains to correct and instruct his hostile adversaries out of compassion and concern for their ignorance and suffering.

Mahatma Gandhi's doctrine of Satyagraha necessarily involved non-violence at all times and in all circumstances.

Because of my Buddhist upbringing I have been a lifelong

pacifist. Needless to say, I am appalled by all the sabre-rattling of world leaders. Why is there such a dearth of articles on the importance of genuine peace that necessarily involves the avoidance of force? It is all very well to denounce terrorism, but how many realise that the use of military power by any state is also a form of terrorism? War is state terrorism. War is legalised murder.

Unfortunately we have been conditioned to think that state terrorism is respectable and justifiable, whereas private terrorism is reprehensible. The violent deeds of individual terrorists are considered morally wrong, but it is morally right for sovereign states to engage in useless wars that inevitably bring death and destruction in their wake! This double standard exists because our minds are confused. Many are suffering from a war psychosis. One wonders whether the eloquent and noble words that form the epigraph to the UNESCO Constitution would ever be heeded: 'Since wars begin in the minds of men, it is in the minds of men that the defences of peace must be constructed.'

It doesn't make the slightest difference to someone who is killed, whether he was put to death by terrorists or by paid soldiers in the employ of a state. Life is our most precious possession. Has the state a moral right even to kill its foes?

Years ago I made a strong protest against the production and sale of arms. What I wrote in *The European* (March 15-17 1991) is directly relevant to all militaristic crises:

> *The real winners of the Gulf War are not the Allies but the manufacturers and sellers of weapons of destruction that stand to make vast profits. Must they not render grateful thanks to their 'peaceful' governments for having permitted this deadly trade? Have not these same governments financially gained by involvement in this dirty business? Weapons manufacture is beastly and unworthy of civilised nations. One of the best ways of discouraging future wars is the imposition of a worldwide ban on the arms trade which, like the slave trade, ought to be regarded as an anachronism. This is not a mere idealistic dream but a very practical means of preventing militarised conflicts.*

Although I am not a Christian, I sometimes turn to the Bible whenever I feel the need for some interesting reading. Must we not take heed of Jesus' advice that condemns all violence? "*Put your sword back in its place,*" instructed Jesus, because "*all who take the sword will die by the sword.*" Furthermore, Jesus asked his followers "*not to take revenge on someone who wrongs you. If anyone slaps you on the right cheek, let him slap your left cheek too.*" Does this not mean that retaliating against any attack is contrary to both the letter and the spirit of Christianity? Now is the time to forgive and forget. Instead of tit-for-tat let us engage ourselves in intense self-searching, sitting quietly and trying to discover why our enemies hate us. We should first of all probe *within* and set our own houses in order.

Bloody conflicts can be avoided if the weaker and poorer states of the world are not forced into accepting the political and economic ideologies of the stronger and richer ones. Why are some states forced into accepting either the Marxist or the capitalist ideology? Will there ever be lasting peace if some countries take it upon themselves to impose fanatically their religious faith on those nations with different beliefs? Why are certain states bullied into accepting democracy as though democracy were a perfect system of government?

We must learn to respect different forms of government. In the same way that, whether we like them or not, we have to accept the existence of monarchical and authoritarian regimes, we have to resign ourselves to the fact that some countries have dictatorships. Not to accept such differences savours of intolerance and any manifestation of intolerance is contrary to the true spirit of democracy.

Several power-hungry, colonialist and world-domineering superpowers seem to suffer from the pathological compulsion to wage wars from time to time. They feel fulfilled only when they are fighting. They are a military threat to countries without nuclear weapons. They create wars, then they enjoy the spoils of wars, next they like to present themselves to the world as peacemakers, and finally they proudly engage themselves in peacekeeping operations! So naturally throughout the world they have all gained notoriety as hypocrites.

How nice if across all the peoples of our planet there is a general consensus about the need for perpetual peace! When more and more people become aware of the horribly painful consequences of war, they will surely start detesting it. In recent times has there been any war without a steady flow of traumatised and homeless refugees? Has there been any war where thousands have not been maimed or massacred? So the question arises as to whether or not our hawkish politicians are sane. Do they deserve to be re-elected? Must we not oust from power all those lethal leaders, those callous killers, who take sadistic pleasure in preparing for wars and participating in them?

Peace is the sole *raison d'être* of the United Nations. The UN was not established to wage wars but to *prevent* them. Is it ethical for statesmen to use the UN as an instrument of war? Belligerent nations would want to use the UN to overthrow the rulers of countries who refuse to be subservient to them. Today the UN is imperilled by such imperious policies. Unfortunately the UN is only a man-made organisation that will always reflect the selfish, aggressive and domineering nature of man. Therefore, instead of pinning our hopes on the UN, the sensible thing would be to purge the mind of its petty nationalism, distrust and hatred of foreigners, racist attitudes, religious fanaticism, violence and such traits that separate one human being from another. We can meditate on the timeless truth enshrined in the epigraph to the UNESCO Constitution: '*Since wars begin in the minds of men, it is in the minds of men that the defences of peace must be constructed.*' Let us therefore turn inwards and ask ourselves whether or not our minds and hearts are pure and conducive to peace.

11

Buddhist Blueprint for World Peace

War is evil.
War is immoral and unethical.
Wars are anachronisms that belong to man's savage past.
A decent and civilised society will have no truck with war.

What actions are necessary to restore a spirit of goodwill in all international relations?

I suggest a blueprint for world peace. Please do not dismiss these proposals as being airy-fairy, for I am only stating the obvious. The world, alas, is becoming increasingly militaristic. Unless we go in the opposite direction our very survival will be at stake. We need a ten-pronged approach to the problem of war and violence:

1. Every country must unhesitatingly abolish her army, navy and air force. She must also stop the production and sale of arms for war and guns for use within the country. A policy of unilateral disarmament by the world's superpowers will be an incentive for all the other nations to do likewise. Similarly, when one by one the rest of the world also starts disarming, these countries will naturally and inevitably feel secure in the knowledge that they no longer need armed forces for their defence and security.
2. Each nation must destroy their arsenals. Nuclear energy, if needed at all, will be used solely for peaceful purposes, and never for the destruction of life.
3. All ex-servicemen and all ex-servicewomen in all countries should be taught new skills so that they can become

genuinely useful members of their communities. Hitherto they had been in the killing profession; henceforth they will lead creative lives in the sense that, instead of being destroyers of life, they will become preservers of it. Those who are too old can become the recipients of retirement pensions. All the scientists and technicians who had hitherto been prostituting their talents and skills by doing research for the creation of increasingly efficient weapons of war, would now, for the first time in their lives, start using their professional knowledge for the economic, social, educational and cultural improvement of mankind.

4. All the scientific laboratories in various states that had up to now been devoted to weapons research will now onwards be used as libraries, galleries, museums and recreational centres.

   Once the world is no longer cursed with war, human beings will have more time and energy to immerse themselves in cultural and intellectual pursuits and, above all, religious pursuits.

5. The United Nations Organisation, instead of being primarily a debating chamber wherein international military conflicts are discussed, will now have a new role. Rather than waste its precious time and energy on military matters, this body will become a platform for the consideration of diverse views relating to the preservation of the environment, flood control, ways and means of preventing droughts, measures for controlling the spread of epidemics and various ecological issues.

   Now onwards there will never be a need to have a Security Council whereby one group of nations is more powerful than the rest. It will be a council of equals. Gone will be the days when the globe was divided into two sections — the bullies and the bullied. Once the world has been purified of the current disease called militarism, a spirit of true friendliness will replace the childish rivalries that unfortunately characterise the UNO today. There will be co-operation in lieu of competition.

6. It would be very naive to believe that, once there are no more wars, human beings will suddenly become gentle and loving, who will coexist in a spirit of selfless brotherhood. The nature of man's psyche is not going to undergo a fundamental change just because a new warless era in world history has suddenly come into existence. It is not that such a radical change can never happen. Such a total transformation will surely occur only when there is a religious metamorphosis, but that is a question that is beyond the scope of this essay, although the attainment of Nirvana is one of the principal themes of this book.
   Human beings will always remain human beings, even in a situation where there are no wars, in the sense that man will continue to be aggressive, envious, spiteful and lacking in compassion. Even so, these nasty traits will never find expression in the form of state-sponsored and state-organised wars, for wars are nothing more than legalised murder. Man, I suppose, in the absence of war, will increasingly resort to participating in various games and sports whereby he can find a release or an outlet for his pugnacity. Instead of having the right to use a gun, it is surely better if a person has the freedom to kick a football with all his or her might.
7. Freed of the fear of getting killed in a war-generated crossfire when people are travelling in different countries, they will have an increased interest in tourism. More and more people will feel at ease when they travel in foreign territories. This practice will, needless to say, broaden the intellectual and cultural horizons of many. Every country will be interested in promoting tourism and cultural exchanges.
8. In a truly civilised world wherein there is lasting peace on earth, more and more students will feel inclined to study overseas. They will have the peace of mind to delve deeply into their special fields of study without the fear of becoming the victims of war and other forms of violence. How seldom do we see that what is called peace of mind is a *sine qua non* for intellectual excellence!

9. The world as a whole will become incalculably richer when there are no more wars. So much of the natural resources of the world, alas, are wantonly wasted at present because being strongly armed at all times has become a senseless obsession with us. There will be remarkable improvements in the standards of living everywhere. Increasingly, the poorer nations might not feel the need to go begging for money and machines. When nations become self-reliant they will naturally feel happier.
10. The former belligerent states of the world have a moral duty to rebuild lands that have had to bear, and still have to bear, the brunt of their ruthless invasions, bombings and terrorist attacks. Nothing can compensate the deaths of thousands of innocent men, women and children. Even so, these once militaristic states must generously help the war-ravaged nations in both cash and kind. When war-mongering states finally give up waging wars, abandoning their pathological involvement in wars once and for all, their wealth will inevitably increase. Money that would normally have been spent on military actions will no longer be frittered away. This means that more than ever before, these countries will now be in a position to pay compensation for their war-inflicted damages.

12

The Buddha Denounced the Destruction of Life

A Brahmin student by the name of Subha went to meet the Buddha who was staying at Savatthi in Jeta's Grove, Anathapindika's Park. After exchanging greetings with him, the student asked Master Gotama, among other things, why human beings are short-lived or long-lived. He was keen on finding out the underlying cause or causes of this inequality. Long was the Buddha's exposition of the subtle ways in which karma operates. The following excerpts from the *Culakammavibhanga Sutta* are confined solely to the consequences of killing:

"Living beings cannot divest themselves
Of their actions.
They are responsible for their actions.
They come into existence because of their actions.
They cannot be separated from their actions.
They take refuge in their actions.
Actions determine one's inferiority or superiority."

"A blood-thirsty and murderous
Man or woman,
Who is aggressive and prone to violence,
Causes the death of a living being.
After that person has passed away,
As a consequence of that misdeed

He will be reborn in a miserable state
With a lack of what is needed,
Even in hell.
But if that person is reborn in human form,
He will not enjoy longevity."

"A man or woman
Gives up the destruction of living beings;
Being kind and gentle,
Casts aside both rod and weapon,
And is filled with compassion
For all living beings.
As a result of such good deeds,
After his demise,
He will be reborn in a happy state,
Even in a celestial realm.
But if after death,
He does not reappear in a happy state,
Or in a celestial realm,
But is reborn in human form,
Then wherever he happens to be,
He will enjoy longevity."

There is a remarkable verse that is not frequently quoted but it is worthy of reflection.

"Whatever a hater might do to a hater,
Or whatever an enemy might do to an enemy,
Our wrongly-directed mind
Will do us greater harm."

— Dhammapada, 42

When is a mind wrongly directed? Whenever there is greed (*Lobha*) we become possessive. The nature of avariciousness is such that it is insatiable. The more we acquire the more we want. Greed is truly an unquenchable thirst.

When it becomes difficult or impossible to acquire the possessions that those who are richer than us have and enjoy, we become envious of them. We get jealous of their success. We start casting covetous eyes at almost anything that is theirs — properties, posh cars, good looks and so forth. Many are jealous of the intelligence, power, prestige, achievements and the like of even their dearest friends and relations. The list of things craved is endless! We feel hate, anger or bitterness (*Dosa*) towards those who are relatively more affluent than us, especially when this unpleasant feeling is compounded by the realisation that we can never reach the same standard as that of our betters.

Soon there are feelings of depression and frustration. Finding oneself relegated to an inferior status is very hurtful. What is it in us that gets hurt? It is the ego. We have been nourishing the delusion (*Moha*) that there is an enduring entity called the 'me' or 'I', which endlessly seeks power, position and glory. Thus the three unwholesome roots of all our problems — greed, hate and delusion keep us in samsaric bondage.

There is no mistaking the cause of suffering — greed, hate and delusion. They are our real enemies, who reside within our minds!

We have long been conditioned to think that we must confront our foes in the external world. Therefore we support the military might of the state. Consequently thousands of human beings are slaughtered in needless wars. Anyone who supports wars becomes a killer by proxy. Such a person inevitably accumulates bad karma.

Looking at the problem from the standpoint of Buddhist philosophy, *there are no external enemies but only internal enemies.* Our only enemies are ourselves. Our real enemies are ourselves. Our *imagined* enemies are other people who get the blame for our difficulties and problems. Our *real* enemies are no other than our stains, traits or tendencies that we carry over from one life to another. Therefore we have no choice but to become our best friends. At present we are our worst enemies. We become our best friends by the inner purification of ourselves.

When men, women and children everywhere start divesting themselves of Greed, Hate and Selfishness (which originates in the delusion that the 'self' is real), hostilities between rival nation states will be seen as an anachronism of our savage past. In such a world there will be neither fierce rivalries between countries nor armed conflicts.

How the primitive love to fight
As though might were morally right!

People compassionate
Never assassinate.

13

Advice on Awareness for Meghiya

The Venerable Meghiya was at one time the personal attendant of the Buddha. Evidently he was a serious-minded monk who received religious instructions from the Buddha. Although the teachings in the *Meghiya Sutta* were given to Meghiya in his capacity as a bhikkhu or monk, they are useful to laypersons as well. The foregoing comment can be made of all other suttas, for laypersons are not precluded from practising the teachings even though a good many of the suttas were speeches given to bhikkhus. In the *Meghiya Sutta*, as we shall see, the requirement to act in accordance with the Patimokkha was specifically aimed at monks.

The *Patimokkha* (Fundamental Precepts) consists of the disciplinary rules to be observed by monks. The Buddha would proclaim a rule when it became necessary to do so in a particular situation. Once a fortnight monks were required to be in conclave and recite their code of conduct. It used to be an occasion for the open confession of violations of the code. Today, however, one monk would confess to another in private, in the belief that they would be purified before their fortnightly meeting.

The Buddha was living among the Calikans on Calika Hill. When Meghiya prostrated before the Buddha and sought permission to go into Jantu Village for almsfood, the Buddha said,

"Yes, Meghiya, do what you think should be done."

Meghiya, after his meal, went for a walk along the banks of the Kimikala River. While taking some exercise in this way, he noticed a pleasant and charming mango grove. Then it occurred to him as follows, "What a pleasing and charming mango grove! How very suitable this grove is for a young man of good family wherein he can meditate! If the Buddha were to grant me permission for it, I would like to use this place for meditation."

When Meghiya requested the Teacher to allow him to take the above-mentioned course of action, the Buddha said,

> *"Since we are alone, Meghiya,*
> *Wait until another monk arrives."*

Meghiya stated, "Revered sir, you have nothing more to do that needs doing, and nothing more to add to what has already been done, but I have something more to do that needs doing, and something more to add to what I have already done. If the Buddha were to grant me permission for it, I would like to use this place for meditation." The Buddha reiterated that Meghiya must wait until some other bhikkhu comes, as they were alone there.

When again Meghiya repeated his request, the Buddha remarked,

> *"Meghiya, what can I say?*
> *Do what you think is best."*

Thereupon Meghiya saluted the Buddha, and entered the mango grove, and proceeded to sit under a tree during the midday rest period. Then Meghiya, while staying there, was deeply troubled by three sorts of thoughts — lustful thoughts, hateful thoughts and cruel thoughts. As these unwholesome thoughts continued to cross his mind, Meghiya started pondering over his plight, "How strange! How marvellous! Although I exchanged home for homelessness, I am still full of unwholesome thoughts — lustful thoughts, hateful thoughts and cruel thoughts." Therefore late in the afternoon Meghiya left his secluded place and went to meet his mentor — the Buddha. Meghiya complained to the Master that he was overpowered by unhealthy thoughts of three kinds — lustful thoughts, hateful thoughts and cruel thoughts.

> *"Meghiya, when awareness*
> *Is still unripe,*

Five things will make it ripen.
What are these?"
"Meghiya, a monk must have
Virtuous friends and associates.
This is the first factor
In the development of awareness."

"Furthermore, Meghiya, a monk must lead
A life of restraint and piety.
In accordance with the Patimokkha,
He must conduct himself rightly,
Seeing danger in the slightest shortcoming.
He should discipline himself to abide by the rules.
This is the second factor
In the development of awareness."

"Meghiya, a monk should also hear
Discourses that are helpful
For the development of awareness —
Talks relating to modesty, seclusion,
Renunciation, dispassion, peace,
Detachment, steadfastness, virtue,
Wisdom and liberation.
This is the third factor
In the development of awareness."

"Meghiya, a monk gives up
Unwholesome states of mind
And has wholesome states of mind.
As regards wholesome states,
He is energetic and persevering.
This is the fourth factor
In the development of awareness."

"In addition, Meghiya, a monk should have
A deep understanding of the rising
And disappearing of things,
Which leads to the complete
Cessation of suffering.

This is the fifth factor
In the development of awareness."

"A monk who has the above-mentioned five qualities,
Should also have the following four —"

"The contemplation of the impurities of the body
For finding freedom from lust;"

"Loving-kindness
For the elimination of ill will;"

"Mindfulness of in-and-out breathing
In order to restrain the stream of thought;"

"And the perception of impermanence
Or the transitoriness of everything
So that the illusion 'I exist' ceases to be.
With the dropping of the 'I'
There is Nirvana in the here and now."

****

"A monk must not regard
What he has received as worthless,
Nor should he be envious of others' gains.
The monk who is given to envying others
Fails to attain insight."

— Dhammapada, 365

"Although the recipient of a little,
If a monk does not dislike what he gets,
Even the celestial beings will praise him,
Provided there is purity of life
And absence of laziness."

— Dhammapada, 366

"When loving-kindness
Characterises a monk's life,
When he gets fulfilment

From the Buddha's teachings,
He attains the tranquil state
Wherein conditioned things
Are no more."

— Dhammapada, 368

References

Anguttara Nikaya : Numerical Discourses of the Buddha selected and translated... Nyanaponika Thera and Bhikkhu Bodhi. Walnut Creek (USA) : AltaMira Press, 1999.

The Buddha and His Teachings by Narada. Colombo : Vajirarama, 1973.

Buddhist Dictionary: A Manual of Buddhist Terms and Doctrines by Nyanatiloka, 3rd edition revised by Nyanaponika. Taipei: Corporate Body of the Buddha Educational Foundation, circa 1987.

The Connected Discourses of the Buddha: A New Translation of the Samyutta Nikaya by Bhikkhu Bodhi. Boston: Wisdom Publications, 2000.

The Dhammapada by F. Max Muller. Delhi: Motilal Banarsidass, 1980, (In *Sacred Books of the East,* vol. 10).

The Dhammapada, translated by K. Sri Dhammananda. Kuala Lumpur: Sasana Abhiwurdhi Wardhana Society, 1992.

Early Buddhist Scriptures : A Selection translated and edited by .Edward J. Thomas. London: Kegan Paul, Trench, Trubner, 1935.

Everyman's Ethics : Four Discourses of the Buddha...translated by Narada. Taipei : Corporate Body of the Buddha Educational Foundation, undated.

The Forest Monks of Sri Lanka... by Michael Carrithers. Delhi : Oxford University Press, 1983.

Great Disciples of the Buddha by Nyanaponika and Helmuth Hecker. Boston: Wisdom Publications, 1997.

The Life of Gotama the Buddha; compiled exclusively from the Pali Canon by E. H. Brewster. London : Routledge & Kegan Paul, 1956.

The Lion's Roar : An Anthology of the Buddha's Teachings selected from the Pali Canon by David Maurice. London: Rider, 1962.

The Middle Length Discourses of the Buddha: A New Translation of the Majjhima Nikaya by Bhikku Nanamoli, edited and revised by Bhikkhu Bodhi. Boston: Wisdom Publications, 1995.

The Pen Portraits of Ninety Three Eminent Disciples of the Buddha by C. De Saram. Colombo: Ceylon Readers Bookshop, 1971.

Psalms of the Early Buddhists: I Psalms of the Sisters by Mrs Rhys Davids. London: Geoffrey Cumberlege for the Pali Text Society, 1948.

Psalms of the Early Buddhists : II Psalms of the Brethren by Mrs Rhys Davids. London : Luzac for the Pali Text Society, 1951.

The Spectrum of Buddhism : Writings of Piyadassi. Taipei : Corporate Body of the Buddha Educational Foundation, 1991.

Thus Have I Heard : The Long Discourses of the Buddha : Digha Nikaya, translated...by Maurice Walshe. London : Wisdom Publications, 1987.

2500 Years of Buddhism, editor P.V. Bapat. New Delhi : Ministry of Information and Broadcasting, 1956.

What Buddhists Believe, 5th edition, by K. Sri Dhammananda. Taiwan: Corporate Body of the Buddha Educational Foundation, 1993.

The Udana: Inspired Utterances of the Buddha, translated...by John D. Ireland. Kandy: Buddhist Publication Society, 1990.

Part II

THE SUTTA NIPATA

Some Selections

Introduction

The *Sutta Nipaṭa* is the oldest book in Buddhist literature.

There is a general consensus among Buddhist scholars about the genuineness of the *Sutta Nipata*. They regard it as a particularly authentic version of the Buddha's teachings because of its great antiquity, language and contents.

I have tried to express the ancient teachings in the idiom of our time. Understanding the teachings correctly is not easy, but putting them into lucid words is even more difficult.

At the end of this part, like the previous one, is the list of References.

I am deeply indebted to the pioneering work of these translators.

14

The Importance of Virtue

Westerners often find it difficult to understand the caste system that prevails in countries such as India or Sri Lanka. In India it is still widely observed whereas in Sri Lanka, owing to their predominantly Buddhist outlook, the people are comparatively less gripped by the power of caste.

Although the origins of the Hindu caste system are lost in the mists of time, we know that historically there have been, and there still are, four main hereditary castes — Brahmin (priests), Kshatriya (warriors), Vaisya (traders) and Sudra (artisans and labourers). The rules and customs of each caste severely restrict the occupations that its members are allowed to choose. Social intercourse with members of other castes is not free and easy but also subject to various rules and customs.

A Sudra is lowborn but still belongs to the fourfold caste system. An outcaste, in contrast, is viewed as an *outsider who does not belong to the caste system.* Thus an outcaste is even less than inferior; he is, in a sense, the lowest of the low. Outcastes are ostracised by society. Mahatma Gandhi and Dr B. R. Ambedkar did much to ease their suffering but there is much more to be done.

Incidentally, all foreigners are, strictly speaking, outcastes as they are outside the caste system and therefore have no secure status in Hindu society.

The horrible stain of untouchability has yet to be eliminated, especially because of the belief that untouchables defile by physically contacting not only food and drink but also by even touching members of high castes. How long are the untouchables going to remain *segregated* in slums and ghettos and condemned to doing degrading menial work such as scavenging?

I had first-hand experience of how the caste system operates in Jaffna when I was the guest of a Shaivite Hindu friend. One morning after we had a refreshing bath in the famous freshwater springs at Keerimalai, we decided to walk along the peaceful palm-fringed beach. My friend, who was in high spirits, started humming mantras. The wide sandy beach was deserted except for a man who was wearing only a loincloth. All of a sudden my friend shouted in Tamil, "Outcaste! Outcaste!" and started chasing the poor man. He slapped the man across the face and kicked him. The frightened stranger took to his heels. "That rascal," said my friend angrily, "has no right to be on the beach, especially when I'm there." This experience was quite upsetting.

It is appalling that in some parts of the Jaffna peninsula, male outcastes never dare to wear any clothes above their waists; if they do, they can expect a savage beating. People punish outcastes who build low walls around their wells, which are safety features. There are many fatalities in the absence of such parapets. Finally, I found that in some villages the children of outcastes were debarred from attending school.

The Hindu caste system results in the separation of people into unfriendly groups. Caste is determined solely by birth, which means that it is not possible to change one's caste. Therefore outcastes are doomed to suffering caused by discrimination against them. They tend to be victimised by persons who belong to so-called high castes. Throughout the ages, has not the caste system been the bane of Asian communities?

I have met proud Westerners, who like to point an accusing finger at caste-ridden Asian societies, deliberately ignoring the fact that there are hardly any Western societies that are not plagued by social divisions based on family, class, wealth, profession, race, religion and the like. There is, for instance, a class system in England that is not fundamentally different from the Indian caste system insofar as one cannot become an aristocrat on one's own merit, because one has to be *born* into an aristocratic family to be regarded as a member of the English aristocracy.

More than 2500 years ago the Buddha denounced the caste system in no uncertain terms. In the *Vasala Sutta* he describes the characteristics that make one an outcaste. The Master explains in so many words that one does not become an outcaste by birth; he specifies the shortcomings, faults or defects, which relegate us to the inferior status of outcastes. By our own bad thoughts and deeds we condemn ourselves. Persons with a theistic background try to put the blame for their moral lapses on an imaginary God, failing to see the simple truth that they alone are responsible for their plight. This discourse on outcastes is about the absence of virtues and the presence of various vices in us.

In the *Vasala Sutta* the Buddha makes it abundantly clear that we become outcastes not by birth, but by whether or not we have a sense of moral rectitude and are paragons of virtue. The Buddha subtly undermines the foundations of Hindu society, as these are unethical and hence unacceptable.

The Buddha was living in the Jeta Grove Monastery of Anathapindika near the city of Savatthi. As was his custom, the Master robed himself one morning, took his begging bowl, and entered the city of Savatthi. While going from house to house on his alms round, he approached the house of a Brahmin called Aggika Bharadvaja.

The Brahmin had kindled the sacred fire and was preparing for his Brahma-Puja or ritual offering. The man was very upset when he saw the Buddha near his house. He was peeved by the Buddha's appearance at an inconvenient hour.

"Remain there you shaveling," the Brahmin remarked rudely, "remain there you miserable monk, remain there you outcaste!"

Despite the man's unwelcoming manner, the Buddha remained unruffled.

"O Brahmin," said the Buddha, "can you recognise an outcaste or the traits that make one an outcaste?"

"No," replied the Brahmin, "it will be good if the Venerable Gotama were to explain me the teachings so that I can not only recognise outcastes but also know their traits."

It is noteworthy that the Brahmin's hostile attitude of mind had instantly disappeared for the man reverentially requested the Buddha to teach him the Dharma.

"Brahmin, please listen attentively," said the Buddha.

"Yes, Venerable One," replied the Brahmin.

Thereupon the Buddha declared that

1. *"Whenever a person is given to anger,*
   Harbours hate,
   Who is vicious and hypocritical,
   Whose perception is perverted
   And who has the habit of deceit
   Look upon him as an outcaste."

2. *"If a person harms living beings,*
   Whether once-born or twice-born,
   And who is devoid of compassion for the living —
   Look upon him as an outcaste."

Creatures that first appear inside eggs are 'twice-born' when the eggs are hatched. Here the Buddha is evidently making a joke of the Brahmins who pride themselves on their 'twice-born' spiritual status.

3. *"Whenever a person is given to destroying*
   And laying siege to villages and towns,
   And is reputed to be hostile —
   Look upon him as an outcaste."

4. *"Be it in village or forest,*
   Whosoever steals others' property,
   Taking what has not been given —
   Look upon him as an outcaste."

5. *"Whenever a debtor denies*
   That he has incurred a debt,
   Avoids his responsibility to repay creditors,
   Saying, 'I owe you nothing' —
   Look upon him as an outcaste."

6. *"Whosoever has a strong desire*
   For a trifling thing belonging to a passer-by,
   Kills him and steals it —
   Look upon him as an outcaste."

7. *"Whosoever when giving evidence as a witness,*
Utters falsehoods out of self-interest,
The interest of others or in order to make a profit —
Look upon him as an outcaste."

8. *"Whosoever, whether forcefully*
Or by mutual consent,
Is seen in the midst of the wives
Of relations or friends —
Look upon him as an outcaste."

9. *"Whenever a wealthy person*
Does not support his parents
Who are no longer young —
Look upon him as an outcaste."

10. *"Whosoever attacks physically*
Or by hurtful words one's mother, father,
Brother, sister or mother-in-law —
Look upon him as an outcaste."

11. *"Whosoever, when asked about*
What is morally good,
Maliciously and deceitfully misleads the inquirer
By counselling the latter to do
What is morally wrong —
Look upon him as an outcaste."

12. *"Whenever a wrongdoer*
Hides his wrongdoing,
And is secretive about his actions —
Look upon him as an outcaste."

13. *"Whosoever partakes of delicious food*
At another's house
But fails to reciprocate,
Not honouring the latter
When he calls on the former —
Look upon him as an outcaste."

14. *"Whosoever tells lies*
And deceives a Brahmin or an ascetic
Or a wandering renunciant —
Look upon him as an outcaste."

15. *"Whosoever uses improper language*
That is intended to upset a Brahmin or an ascetic
Who visits him at meal-time,
And fails to offer alms to the mendicant —
Look upon him as an outcaste."

16. *"Whosoever, being steeped in ignorance,*
Makes forecasts that are untrue
In order to acquire something —
Look upon him as an outcaste."

17. *"Whosoever praises himself,*
Being debased by pride,
And looks down on others —
Look upon him as an outcaste."

18. *"Whosoever is given to anger, greed,*
Prone to wrongdoing;
Who is jealous, evil-minded, shameless
And not afraid of doing what is morally wrong —
Look upon him as an outcaste."

19. *"Whosoever speaks abusively of the Buddha*
Or any follower of the Master
(Be he a wandering ascetic who lives on alms
Or a layperson) —
Look upon him as an outcaste."

20. *"Whosoever pretends to be an Arhat,*
Without actually being one,
Is a thief in the entire universe,
Including the world of Brahman.
He is in fact the lowest of the outcaste."

"The persons I have described to you are all outcastes."

21. *"Whether or not one is an outcaste*
Is never determined by birth.
Whether or not one is a Brahmin
Is never determined by birth.
It is by deeds that one is an outcaste;
It is by deeds that one is a Brahmin."

22. *"I cite the example of Sopaka,*
The son of an outcaste,
Who became well known as Matanga."

23. *"This Matanga attained the greatest fame,*
Which was so difficult to achieve.
Many warriors and Brahmins served him."

24. *"He got into the heavenly chariot*
(Noble Eightfold Path)
And drove along the lust-free road.
Having given up sense-desires,
He reached the Brahma realm."

25. *"His humble origins*
Did not get in the way
Of his being reborn
In the Brahma realm,
Yet there are Brahmins,
Born in the family of teachers,
Friends of Vedic hymns —"

26. *"Who are given to doing evil deeds.*
They are blameworthy in this world.
After death they go to unhappy states.
Their so-called high birth
Neither protects them
From rebirth in a woeful state
Nor from blame."

27. *"Not by birth is one an outcaste.*
Not by birth is one a Brahmin.
By deeds one becomes an outcaste.
By deeds one becomes a Brahmin."

"Excellent, O Venerable Gotama, excellent!" exclaimed the Brahmin Aggika Bharadvaja, who had been patiently listening to the Buddha's discourse. "The Venerable Gotama in many ways has explained the Dharma," he said, "revealing what had hitherto been hidden, showing the right direction to those who have gone astray, holding an oil lamp for the benefit of those who are shrouded in darkness. I take refuge in the Buddha, the Dharma and the Sangha. May the Venerable Gotama accept me as a lay disciple until the end of my days."

Kusinara in India has become a famous place of pilgrimage. It was here in a grove of sala trees that the Buddha passed away.

Subhadda, the wandering ascetic, was staying at Kusinara. On hearing that the Buddha's *Parinirvana* would take place that night, Subhadda rushed to meet the Master, but the Venerable Ananda tried to dissuade Subhadda from going ahead with his plan. The Buddha, after overhearing their conversation about this matter, agreed to meet the ascetic who wanted to pose three questions that were troubling him. He had already approached other religious teachers but their answers to these questions did not satisfy Subhadda.

These were his questions:

1. In the sky are there tracks?
2. Outside the Buddhist community, are there any who have attained Nirvana?
3. Is there any conditioned thing (*Sankhara*) that has permanency?

The Buddha's answers to all three questions were in the negative.

'Pathless is the sky.
Outside no Saints can be found.
No conditioned thing is everlasting.
The Buddhas have ceased moving.'

— Dhammapada, 255

15

What is Conducive to Happiness ?

In the Buddhist world an immensely popular sutta is the *Maha Mangala Sutta*. It is often recited when people gather for the purpose of listening to *paritta* chanting in temples, public halls or homes.

The title of this sutta has been misleadingly translated as 'Discourse on Blessings' and all the stanzas end with the recurring statement 'this is the highest blessing'. Blessings are special favours, benefits or gifts bestowed by God or a deity upon recipients that bring the latter happiness. Since the word 'blessings' has theistic connotations, I have used instead the term 'conducive to happiness' when referring to 'mangala'. Apart from 'conducive to happiness', the word 'mangala' can also mean 'auspicious', 'lucky' or 'good omen'.

The pathological belief that there might be a higher power that bestows blessings, and even the very belief in blessings, are quite contrary to the teachings of the Buddha, who made it very clear that each person must all alone, that is to say single-handedly, extricate himself or herself from the burden of karma and recurrent births. Let us meditate on his famous teaching:

> *"Atta hi attano natho*
> *Ko hi natho paro siya"*
>
> *"Man is his own saviour.*
> *Who else could be the saviour?"*
>
> — The Dhammapada, 160

The Buddha delivered a lecture on the factors determining happiness at the monastery of Anathapindika near Savatthi. To devotees of the Dharma, the name Anathapindika conjures up images of important events in the life of the Buddha. The great philanthropist Anathapindika, or 'one who provides alms for the needy', constructed a monastery in a park and presented it to the Buddha, who spent nineteen rainy seasons there. It was in this monastery that the Teacher lived an important part of his life and delivered many lectures.

Once when it was quite late at night a certain beautiful deity, whose radiance was so bright that it illuminated the entire Jeta Grove, approached the Teacher and saluted him deferentially. The deity addressed the Buddha as follows:

1. *"Many persons and celestial beings have been carefully considering this matter but it still remains unresolved. Please tell me what factors are conducive to finding happiness."*

2. *"Not associating with fools*
   But associating with the clear-sighted,
   And honouring those
   Deserving of honour —
   This is conducive to happiness."

3. *"Living in suitable surroundings,*
   To have done meritorious deeds in the past,
   And inquiring into oneself
   Attentively, carefully and completely —
   This is conducive to happiness."

4. *"Having great erudition and skill,*
   Exercising self-restraint,
   And telling the truth —
   This is conducive to happiness."

'Great erudition' refers to a good knowledge of the Dharma. 'Skill' denotes the doing of good deeds that cause no injury whatsoever to any living being; it excludes, needless to say, any behaviour that is not righteous.

5. *"Taking care of one's father and mother,*
Providing for one's wife and children,
And right livelihood —
This is conducive to happiness."

6. *"Giving generously to the poor,*
Living righteously,
Helping relations,
And being blameless in one's actions —
This is conducive to happiness."

'Living righteously' becomes possible by observing the Five Precepts — neither killing nor causing to kill any living creature, never making untrue statements, avoiding unlawful sexual activity, refraining from stealing or the taking of that which has not been given; and finally, the virtue of temperance.

7. *"Stopping the doing of evil deeds,*
And refraining from them,
Eschewing alcohol and intoxicants,
And being unwaveringly virtuous or morally excellent —
This is conducive to happiness."

'Mind-expanding' drugs and other hallucinogenic substances probably fall into the category of alcohol.

8. *"The qualities of being respectful,*
Humble, contented, grateful
As well as being attentive to the Dharma
At the right time —
This is conducive to happiness."

9. *"Patience and sweetness,*
The sight of recluses
And discussions about the Dharma
At the right time —
This is conducive to happiness."

The word '*sovacassata*', which literally means 'suavity' is here construed as sweetness or pleasantness.

10. *"Morality, sexual purity,*
Understanding the Noble Truths
And the attainment of Nirvana —
This is conducive to happiness."

11. *"A mind that maintains its composure*
After coming into contact with mundane matters,
Free from suffering and defilements,
And having no fear —
This is conducive to happiness."

The liberated Arhat is totally untouched by gain and loss, honour and dishonour, praise and blame, joy and sorrow.

12. *"Those who have accomplished*
Doing these things
Are triumphant in every way,
They walk in safety everywhere —
This is conducive to happiness."

16

Causes of Our Decline and Fall

In many countries it is customary to regard the Buddha as a great religious teacher, though in the Buddhist world he is respected and revered as *the greatest* religious teacher — the fully Awakened One. The Buddha was, in addition, an outstandingly profound social philosopher whose social teachings can be traced back to his wellspring of loving concern for humanity. He was, however, very different from other social philosophers in so far as social problems were not viewed by him as being fundamentally different from the problems of the human psyche. He knew that healing the wounds within the mind was the indispensable and the preliminary requisite for solving all social problems. That is to say, by individually discovering the cause of one's suffering (*Dukkha*), and thereby extricating oneself from it, one automatically finds the solutions to each and every social problem. Without reforming ourselves first, is it really possible to reform society? It is absolutely necessary to rid ourselves of the popular myth that we are basically different from the societies wherein we dwell. The society in which we live is acquisitive and competitive only because we ourselves are acquisitive and competitive. Even in ancient times the Greek philosophers viewed the state as nothing more than a magnification of the individual.

Many Marxist theoreticians failed to see that man must change first before their utopia comes into existence. Marxist thinkers have offered blueprints for a perfect and moral society, ignoring the fact that achieving a utopian classless society by force entails a bloody revolution — violence and the liquidation of political opponents. Is there anything more immoral than killing?

There is a Marxist belief that an ethical society can only happen in a socialist society. After the 1917 Russian Revolution, did the men, women and children of that country suddenly become altruistic angels? Did the basic avariciousness of the communist citizens disappear for good? Did the residents of Russia *change* deeply and psychologically in the sense that they were no longer given to anger and hate (*Dosa*)? The Bolshevik system resulted in a more egalitarian society but human nature, alas, remained unchanged. The commissars who ruled the country were as power-hungry and ruthless as their capitalistic predecessors. Revolutions only bring about outer changes in the fabric of society but the inner beast within man, so to speak, remains not only unchanged but also untamed.

It can of course be argued that without resorting to a violent political and economic revolution, it would be possible to introduce gradually and by peaceful democratic means an economy that is based on the public ownership of the means of production and distribution. Yes, that is certainly possible, but can there ever be a perfect social system so long as we are greedy, acquisitive and enslaved by craving or 'psychological thirst' (*Tanha*), which is the principal cause of suffering?

The Buddha has drawn our attention to the truth that first of all the individuals who make up society must have a completely reformed character before there can ever be any significant social change. 'Society' is only a collective term that we use to denote the individuals that comprise it, which means that misbehaviour on the part of various individuals will always result in social degradation. In wartime, for instance, we like to lay the blame on governments that pursue militaristic policies. We conveniently forget that, whether or not we had voted in the belligerent governments in power, the truth of the matter is that we ourselves in our lives are not totally free from resentments, aggressiveness and violence. Why do we fail to realise that the *casus belli* (grounds for war) or real root of war is our hateful mindset?

The *Parabhava Sutta* is about the twelve main reasons for man's downfall in the world. The day after the Buddha's discourse on *What is Conducive to Happiness* (Maha Mangala Sutta), the celestial beings requested the Master to teach them about the things that bring about their decline and fall.

The Buddha was in residence at Anathapindika's monastery near Savatthi. It was late in the night when a certain beautiful celestial being visited him. The radiance of the deity brightened up the entire place. The deity respectfully greeted the Master, stood near him, and posed a question about why a man suffers loss: What causes his downfall?

The Buddha delivered a discourse as follows:

1. *"Easily recognisable is the winner;*
   Easily recognisable is the loser.
   The lover of the Dharma wins;
   The hater of the Dharma loses."

2. *"He finds the wicked endearing;*
   His deeds are not endearing to the good;
   He accepts the teachings of the wicked —
   This results in his downfall."

3. *"Feeling drowsy, he is almost asleep,*
   Enjoys the company of others,
   Listless, lazy and irritable —
   This results in his downfall."

Apart from moral lassitude (lack of interest), there are physical factors that can also cause drowsiness — undernourishment, heavy eating and drinking, fatigue, lack of sleep, excessive sleep, the after-effects of drugs, oxygen deprivation and the lack of exercise.

4. *"Whoever being wealthy,*
   Does not help his aged parents,
   Who have passed their prime —
   This results in his downfall."

5. *"He who tells lies and thereby deceives*
   A Brahmin or an ascetic

Or any other person living on alms —
This results in his downfall."

6. *"The man who owns many properties,*
Including gold and food,
But enjoys his sweet possessions all alone —
This results in his downfall."

7. *"The man who takes pride in his birth,*
His riches and his family,
But much dislikes his relations —
This results in his downfall."

8. *"A promiscuous man*
Who is an alcoholic and a gambler
Given to spending his earnings wastefully —
This results in his downfall."

9. *"Not content with having his own wives,*
A man is seen with others' wives and prostitutes —
This results in his downfall."

Provided he had the means to support them, a man in the days of the Buddha was permitted to have more than one wife. Extramarital affairs were frowned upon at that time.

10. *"When a man, who is no longer young,*
Brings home a female
With breasts similar to timbaru fruits,
But he cannot sleep
Out of jealousy of her —
This results in his downfall."

His insomnia probably originates in the fear that she might prefer a younger lover to him.

11. *"He who places in a position*
Of power and authority
Either a man or a woman
Who not only takes alcohol
But is also given to using money

Carelessly and foolishly —
This results in his downfall."

12. *"When a poor person of warrior birth*
Is very ambitious
And craves for kingship in this world —
This results in his downfall.'

'Understanding the causes
Of decline and fall in the world,
The wise and venerable sage of great insight
Enjoys a happy realm."

"Hunger is the worst disease.
Combined things are the greatest of sorrows.
Understanding this as an actual fact
Is Nirvana, the highest happiness."
— Dhammapada, 203

Here 'hunger' refers to greed or craving.

The 'combined things' are the five constituent parts, which collectively create the illusion of 'a being', 'I' or 'self'.

The five aggregates are:

The body	*Rupa*
Feelings	*Vedana*
Perception	*Sanna*
Mental states	*Sankhara*
Consciousness	*Vinnana*

17

Demons Discuss the Buddha's Great Qualities

The Buddha was a great magnet for humans and non-humans. The Yakkhas are one of the classes of non-humans who listened to the Buddha's discourses. Some of the Yakkhas are seen as harmful demons, but others are guardians of the teachings. The latter are regarded as protectors of the Dharma. A tradition has grown up that Yakkhas live in the air but some on land. Be that as it may, we ought to consider an interesting conversation that two Yakkhas had about the Buddha's qualities. Thereafter they decided to visit him.

It was during the darkness of the night that the two Yakkhas met, when the Yakkha Satagira expressed the wish to meet the Teacher. Their timing was not without significance. For it was in the course of the Middle Watch in the Buddha's daily routine, which extended from 10 p.m. to 2 a.m., that celestial beings such as Devas and other beings, who are invisible to ordinary persons, approached the Buddha to discuss questions relating to the Dharma.

The *Hemavatasutta* starts with a dialogue between Yakkha Satagira and Yakkha Hemavata.

Satagira: "Today is the fifteenth and a fast-day. What a beautiful night! Shall we visit the famous Master Gotama?"

Hemavata: "Has his mind a favourable disposition towards all beings? Has his mind a sense of detachment from what is pleasant and what is unpleasant?"

Satagira: "His mind is favourably disposed towards all beings, and it also has a sense of detachment from what is pleasant and what is unpleasant."

Hemavata: "Does he not take what has not been offered? Does he desist from harming living beings? Is he free from carelessness? Is he not negligent in meditation?"

Satagira: "He does not take what has not been offered. He desists from harming living beings. He is free from carelessness. The Buddha is not negligent in meditation."

Hemavata: "Does he not tell lies? Does he not use bad language? Is he not a slanderer? Does he not say things that are untrue or stupid?"

Satagira: "He does not tell lies. He does not use bad language. He is not a slanderer. He does not say things that are untrue or stupid. He says things that are sensible."

Hemavata: "Does he not crave for sensual pleasures? Is his mind peaceful? Has he transcended delusion? As regards mental phenomena, has he clarity of vision?"

Satagira: "He is not attached to sensual pleasures. His mind is peaceful. He has gone beyond delusion. As regards mental phenomena, the Buddha has clarity of vision."

Hemavata: "Has he knowledge? Are his actions pure? Have his desires died? Will he not be reborn?"

Satagira: "He has knowledge. His conduct is pure.
His passions have disappeared. He will never be reborn."

"The mind of the great sage is perfect in word and deed.
Let us go and see Gotama."

"Come, let us visit Gotama, whose legs look like those of an antelope, who is slim, who has wisdom, who eats frugally, who is not covetous, the mighty Seer who meditates in the forest."

"After meeting this lion-like being, this solitary wanderer, who seeks not sensual pleasures, let us ask him about freedom from Death's trap."

"Let us together ask Gotama, the preacher, who has gone to the other shore, the Buddha who has rid himself of hatred and fear."

Hemavata: "In what has the world come into existence? By being attached to what does the world exist? In what way is the world troubled?"

The Buddha: *"The world originated in six things.*
It is supported by six factors.
The world is troubled in six ways."

Hemavata: "What is that grasping which troubles the world? How can one find an end to sorrow?"

The Buddha: *"In the world*
The five pleasures of the senses
Are in operation
Along with the pleasure of the mind.
With the dropping of the desire for these,
Sorrow ends."
"The salvation of the world
Has been truthfully explained to you.
I tell you that in this manner
One extricates oneself from sorrow."

Hemavata: "Who in this world passes the samsaric stream? Who in this world passes the ocean? Who does not drown in the sea wherein there is neither a place for standing nor any support?"

The Buddha: *"The stream*
That is not easy to cross
Can be traversed by him
Who is virtuous and wise,
Quiet and calm,
Who is inward-watching,

Aware and observant of himself."

"He does not get drowned
Who treats sensual pleasures
With complete indifference,
Who removes the obstacles,
And no longer yearns for life,
Not enchained by becoming."

Hemavata: "See the Seer with penetrating intelligence, who understands what is subtle, who owns nothing, who is unattached to the pleasures of the senses and free from becoming, absolutely free in every respect, and who treads the celestial way!"

"See the Seer of great repute, who notices what is not easy to see, who gives understanding, who is unsullied by lust, the knower of all things, the supremely intelligent one, who treads the noble way!"

All the Yakkhas: "Today we had a good sight. The break of dawn was good. Beautiful was the rising, for we have seen the fully-Awakened One, who has gone across the stream, and who is without taints and pure."

"We are a thousand famous Yakkhas with supernatural powers. We all take refuge in you — our Master beyond compare."

"With reverence for the Enlightened One and the perfect Dharma, we shall walk around from village to village and from mountain to mountain."

"Difficult is birth in human form.
Difficult is the life of mortals.
Difficult is the hearing of the Pure Dharma.
Difficult is the coming into being of the Buddhas."

— Dhammapada, 182

"Not doing anything bad,
Doing good,

Purifying the mind —
This is the teaching of the Buddhas."

— Dhammapada, 183

"Patience is the principal penance.
Nirvana is the highest, the Awakened proclaim.
He, truly, is not a monk who is cruel to another,
Nor is he an ascetic who annoys others."

— Dhammapada, 184

18

The Demon Alavaka Challenges the Buddha

All manner of men and women, including invisible beings, thronged to see the Buddha and hear him speak. Taking into consideration the fact that the appearance of a Buddha in our world is such a rarity, it must be said that those who met the Buddha and knew him personally were privileged indeed.

It is reasonable to assume that one does not, and indeed cannot, meet a Buddha by chance. Such an extraordinary event does not take place because of a purely fortuitous or accidental combination of circumstances. What is the traditional view? It is only because of one's past good karma that one comes into contact with a Buddha.

Powerful kings and wealthy aristocrats were among those who enjoyed having the company of the Buddha. Probably it was the case that some were keen on hobnobbing with the Buddha in expectation of basking in the reflected glory of the famous Sage. On the whole people were friendly towards him. But some were envious of him. They felt hatred for the Buddha. Even so noble and great a personality, alas, was not without enemies.

Often the Buddha had to face confrontations with persons who were hostile to him. His adversaries frequently took a strange and mischievous delight in challenging him. They got much pleasure out of verbal duels. They liked to pit their wits against those of the Master. Many were the reasons why they relished debating with him. There were, for example, learned Brahmins and the leaders of religious sects whose religious and philosophical views widely diverged from those of the Buddha. They felt that they had to argue out their concepts, for they were fearful that the Buddha was shattering the very foundations of their settled ideologies and cherished beliefs. Consequently they started having feelings of insecurity.

Sometimes people approached the Buddha on the pretext of asking him questions, but what they really wanted to do was to humiliate him, and thereby give expression to their lurking pugnacity and aggressiveness. In such situations, did the Buddha take revenge on his enemies? Did he retaliate against those who made scathing attacks on him and his teachings? On the contrary, he held his opponents in deep affection. Extracting an eye for an eye or a tooth for a tooth was never the Buddha's way of treating people who had little or no respect for him. Whenever the Buddha was insulted, neither did he lose his composure nor his temper. With infinite patience and compassion he would show the defeated debaters the mistakes in their minds. Foes became friends. Never has there been a better travel guide than the Buddha, who guided the worrying world through the path of purity and showed the ending of human suffering.

The *Alavakasutta* is about the Yakkha Alavaka, the deplorable demon who later became a devoted disciple of the Buddha.

The Buddha was residing in Alavi. At that time Alavi was under the control of a demon called the Yakkha Alavaka. After having gone to the place where the Buddha was staying, Alavaka said,

> "Come out, O recluse!"
>
> "*Yes, sir,*" said the Buddha, as he came out.
>
> "Go inside, O recluse!" said the Yakkha.
>
> "*Yes, sir,*" said the Buddha, as he went inside.
>
> "Come out, O recluse!" the Yakkha ordered for the second time.
>
> "*Yes, sir,*" said the Buddha, as he came out.
>
> "Go inside, O recluse!' said the Yakkha.
>
> "*Yes, sir,*" said the Buddha, as he went inside.
>
> "Come out, O recluse!" the Yakkha ordered for the third time.

"*Yes, sir,*" said the Buddha, as he came out.
"Go inside, O recluse!' said the Yakkha.
"*Yes, sir,*" said the Buddha, as he went inside.

"Come out, O recluse!" the Yakkha ordered for the fourth time.
"*I shall not go out for you, sir. Do what you please,*" replied the Buddha.

Alavaka: "O recluse! I will ask you a question and if you don't answer, I will make you so confused that you will not be able to think properly, or I will tear your heart out, or I will grab your feet and fling you over the Ganges River."

The Buddha: *"Sir, I don't see anyone in this world*
Nor in the celestial world of gods,
Including Mara and Brahma,
As well as recluses, Brahmins and other beings,
Who could do any of the things
That you have just mentioned.
Nevertheless, sir, ask what you like."

Thereupon the Yakkha addressed the Buddha in verse.

Alavaka: "In this world what wealth is best?
What, when well done, brings happiness?
What is the sweetest of the sweet?
What way of living is the best?"

The Buddha: *"In this world the best wealth is faith.*
Living the Dharma brings happiness.
The sweetest of the sweet is truth.
Living with understanding is the best life."

Alavaka: "How does one cross the stream of samsara?
How does one cross the deep?
How does one put a stop to suffering?
How does one find the state of purity?"

The Buddha: *"By means of faith one crosses samsara.*
By means of vigilance one crosses the deep.

By means of vigour suffering ends.
By means of understanding there is purification."

Alavaka: "How is understanding found?
How are riches found?
How is fame found?
How are friends bound together?
How does one remain griefless
when departing from this world?"

The Buddha: *"There is understanding,*
When one has faith in the Dharma of the Arhats
Regarding the attainment of Nirvana,
Being perseveringly attentive and insightful.'

'One acquires wealth by doing what is right
And by setting oneself to work.
Through truth one finds fame.
Generosity ties friends to each other."

"The faithful householder
Has the following four virtues —
Truth, Morality (Dharma),
Steadfastness and Liberality or Generosity.
Such a person is without grief
When he or she is breathing his last."

"Go over great distances
And ask other recluses and Brahmins
If in this world there is anything
That is higher than Truth,
Restraint, Liberality or Generosity,
And Forbearance or Reluctance to Retaliate."

Alavaka: "Why must I seek the advice of recluses and Brahmins? Today I already know what is good for me."

"For my benefit the Buddha came to stay at Alavi. I now know that the given gift will bear abundant fruit."

"I will move around from village to village and from town to town, replete with veneration for the fully-Awakened One and the perfect Dharma."

"People make donations
In proportion to their faith
And their gratification.
Those who worry about the food and drink
That they give to others
Have no peace of mind
Either by day
Or by night."

— Dhammapada, 249

"When in a person
This feeling has vanished
Without trace,
When it has been totally uprooted,
He finds peace of mind
By day
And by night."

— Dhammapada, 250

19

Dropping the Inner Obstacles

The sense of Liberation or Freedom from the burden of karma in the *Uragasutta* is conveyed in the final words of every stanza — "like a snake that leaves behind its worn-out skin". Letting the worn-out skin drop is symbolic of dropping the inner blemishes or taints. It signifies the state of purity.

1. *"The monk who allows his anger*
   To disappear when it arises,
   In the same way that one allows
   Herbs to detoxify a snake-poisoned body,
   Such a monk leaves behind this shore
   And the shore beyond.
   He is like a snake that leaves behind its worn-out skin."

2. *"The monk who cuts himself off completely*
   From the sway of passion,
   In the same way that one dives into the water
   And cuts off the stalk of a lotus,
   Severing both stalk and flower from the plant,
   Such a monk leaves behind this shore
   And the shore beyond.
   He is like a snake that leaves behind its worn-out skin."

3. *"The monk who completely*
   Does away with craving,
   This drying up of the rapidly rushing river,
   Such a monk leaves behind this shore

And the shore beyond.
He is like a snake that leaves behind its worn-out skin."

4. *"The monk who fully roots up pride,*
Like a forceful flood
That washes away a shaky bridge of reeds,
Such a monk leaves behind this shore
And the shore beyond.
He is like a snake that leaves behind its worn-out skin."

5. *"The monk who has not found anything*
Of importance in the cycle of births,
Like not finding flowers among fig-trees,
Such a monk leaves behind this shore
And the shore beyond.
He is like a snake that leaves behind its worn-out skin."

6. *"The monk who harbours no resentments,*
Who for this reason will not be reborn,
Such a monk leaves behind this shore
And the shore beyond.
He is like a snake that leaves behind its worn-out skin."

7. *"The monk, whose doubts have disappeared,*
Being deeply detached within,
Such a monk leaves behind this shore
And the shore beyond.
He is like a snake that leaves behind its worn-out skin."

8. *"The monk who is neither too fast nor too slow,*
Who has transcended delusion,
Such a monk leaves behind this shore
And the shore beyond.
He is like a snake that leaves behind its worn-out skin."

The expression 'neither too fast nor too slow' is suggestive of a way of life that avoids the two extremes — working so intensely, restlessly and too austerely that one neglects the body and consequently falls ill, and the other extreme of being too relaxed and lethargic that it borders on laziness. Evidently, it is the middle way that is recommended.

9. *"The monk who is neither too fast nor too slow,*
Who having realised that the world is false
And that all is unreal,
Such a monk leaves behind this shore
And the shore beyond.
He is like a snake that leaves behind its worn-out skin."

10. *"The monk who is neither too fast nor too slow,*
Being free from greed,
Who realises that the world is false
And that all is unreal,
Such a monk leaves behind this shore
And the shore beyond.
He is like a snake that leaves behind its worn-out skin."

11. *"The monk who is neither too fast nor too slow,*
Being devoid of passion,
Who realises that the world is false
And that all is unreal,
Such a monk leaves behind this shore
And the shore beyond.
He is like a snake that leaves behind its worn-out skin."

12. *"The monk who is neither too fast nor too slow,*
Being liberated from hatred,
Who realises that the world is false
And that all is unreal,
Such a monk leaves behind this shore
And the shore beyond.
He is like a snake that leaves behind its worn-out skin."

13. *"The monk who has no fear-based traits whatsoever*
That result in rebirth,
Such a monk leaves behind this shore
And the shore beyond.
He is like a snake that leaves behind its worn-out skin."

14. *'The monk who has no desire-based traits whatsoever*
That cause enslavement to samsara,
Such a monk leaves behind this shore

And the shore beyond.
He is like a snake that leaves behind its worn-out skin."

15. *"The monk who having managed*
To surmount the five obstacles,
Is free from sorrow,
And who, having gone beyond doubt,
No longer suffers pain.
Such a monk leaves behind this shore
And the shore beyond.
He is like a snake that leaves behind its worn-out skin."

In Buddhist literature there are recurring references to the five obstacles. Many are the obstacles but there are five main ones. What are they? They are termed the five hindrances or Nivarnas.

Nivarnas

The obstacles are as follows:

Sensuous desire	*Kamacchanda*
Ill-will	*Vyapada*
Sloth and Torpor	*Thina – middha*
Restlessness and worry	*Uddhacca – kukkucca*
Sceptical doubt	*Vicikiccha*

The Arhat has transcended all these and more.

"Cast aside the future,
Cast aside the past,
Cast aside the present,
When you cross the stream to the other shore,
Your mind being fully free,
There will never again be birth nor decay."

— Dhammapada, 348

20

Rich Dhaniya Talks to the Buddha

In the *Dhaniyasutta* a wealthy herdsman by the name of Dhaniya talks about himself rather boastfully when he has a conversation with the Buddha.

Dhaniya: "I have boiled my rice and finished my milking. By the banks of the Mahi River I live with my companions. My house is roofed and the fire is lit. So, O sky-deva, if you wish, rain!"

The Buddha: *"I have no anger and my mind*
Is free from callousness.
For one night I stay
Near the banks of the Mahi River.
My house is roofless.
My fire is not burning.
So, O sky-deva, if you wish, rain!"

'My house is roofless' probably refers to the recluse who lives without the shelter of any house. It could also refer to the unconditioned state of openness of the truly Liberated Ones. 'My fire is not burning' could similarly refer to the karma-less state wherein all the fires of desire are no more.

Dhaniya: "There are no gadflies here. In the lush grassy fields the cows are grazing. They can endure rain if it comes. So, O sky-deva, if you wish, rain!"

The Buddha: *"There is a well-timbered raft.*
Having crossed over the flood
That sweeps one away from Liberation,
I have reached the further shore of Nirvana.
I need the raft no more.
So, O sky-deva, if you wish, rain!"

Dhaniya: "Attentive is my wife, not loose. She has been with me for long. She is nice. I hear nothing bad of her. So, O sky-deva, if you wish, rain!"

The Buddha: *"Attentive is my mind, fully free.*
Over a long time it has been well tamed.
No longer is there anything
Unwholesome in me.
So, O sky-deva, if you wish, rain!"

Dhaniya: "I am self-supporting. My sons who are living with me enjoy good health. I hear nothing bad of them. So, O sky-deva, if you wish, rain!"

The Buddha: *"I am not the servant of anyone.*
With my own earnings
I wander in the world.
I need no wage.
So, O sky-deva, if you wish, rain!"

Dhaniya: "I have cows, calves, pregnant cows, heifers as well as a bull that lords it around the cows. So, O sky deva, if you wish, rain!"

The Buddha: *"I have no cows,*
No calves,
No pregnant cows,
No heifers and
No bull that lords it around the cows.
So, O sky-deva,if you wish, rain!"

Dhaniya: "The stakes are firmly grounded and unshakeable. The munga grass ropes are new and of such high quality that the cows cannot break them.
So, O sky-deva, if you wish, rain!"

The Buddha: *"Like a bull that breaks its bonds,*
Like an elephant that tears a creeper apart,
Never again will I enter into a womb.
So, O sky-deva, if you wish, rain!"

All of a sudden there was a heavy shower that filled both the low-lying lands and the high.

On hearing the sound of the rain, Dhaniya declared, "Great is our gain after seeing the Buddha! O great Sage, be our teacher, we seek refuge in you, O Seer!"

"Both my wife and I are attentive. We shall lead the holy life before the Happy One. We shall terminate the cycle of births and deaths and end suffering."

Mara
(the Evil One): "He who has sons takes delight in having sons. He who has cows takes delight in having cows. For attachment is man's source of delight. But the one without attachments has gone beyond the need for delight."

The Buddha: *"One with sons will grieve over his sons.*
One with cows will grieve over his cows.
For attachment,
Is the source of man's grief.
But the one without attachments,
Being carefree, never grieves."

While on his way to the Deer Park in Varanasi to deliver his first sermon, the Buddha's radiance so impressed a wandering ascetic called Upaka that he approached the Master and asked, "who is your teacher? What is your doctrine?"

"All I have conquered,
All I do know,
From all I am detached,
All I have cast aside,
From all stains I am free.
Having understood

By myself alone,
Who really is my teacher?"

— Dhammapada, 353

"The gift of the Dharma
Exceeds all other gifts.
The flavour of the Dharma
Exceeds all other flavours.
The delight in the Dharma
Exceeds all other delights.
The cessation of craving
Is the victory over all sorrow."

— Dhammapada, 354

21

Four Kinds of Recluses

Recluses can be described as persons who for whatever reason live in seclusion. Do fugitives from justice or outlaws who feel the need to live in their hide-outs also fall into the category of recluses? In a sense they do, but in this discussion we are only concerned with recluses who live alone for religious reasons, especially for undisturbed meditation in quiet surroundings.

Monks who are forest dwellers might avoid meeting people altogether on principle. Even monks forming part of a monastic community often limit their social lives to an absolute minimum of contact with human beings. When monks beg for alms they hardly speak with those who offer them food. What criteria should one use to judge whether or not a monk is a real recluse? Is it a question of whether he lives amidst people or away from them? It seems to me that a genuine recluse forms no attachments to anybody or anything. He is, in other words, a true renunciant or at least aspires to be one.

Although the *Kundasutta* is very short in length, it is very rich in wisdom. The smith Kunda asked the Buddha to clarify his position on recluses.

Kunda: "I request the Sage of vast wisdom, who has gone beyond craving, who is the foremost of the two-legged and the champion charioteer, to answer this question. In the world how many kinds of recluses are there?"

The Buddha: *"There are four kinds of recluses,*
There is no fifth, O Kunda."

The Buddha proceeded to describe the four categories:

First, the recluses who know the way.
Second, the recluses who teach the way.
Third, the recluses who live the way.
Fourth, the recluses who desecrate the way.

The Buddha: *"He who has dropped doubts*
And is free from suffering,
Who finds delight in Nirvana
And is craving-free,
Who guides gods and men,
Such a person (Maggagina)
Is a ***knower of the way.****"*

"He who in this world has realised
The Highest as the Highest (Nirvana)
And teaches the Dharma,
This craving-free
And doubt-destroying Sage (Maggadesin)
Is a ***teacher of the way.****"*

"He who lives by the teachings,
The texts of the Dharma,
Who is disciplined, attentive
And follows the pure paths,
Such a person (Maggagivin),
Is a ***liver of the way.****"*

"He who pretends to be virtuous
Is a disgrace to families.
He is a deceitful
And undisciplined hypocrite
Who is given to talking idly.
Such a person (Maggadusin)
Is a ***desecrater of the way.****"*

"When a householder fully understands
These four types of recluses,

Seeing them exactly as they are,
Such a person's faith does not get badly shaken.
How could he possibly mistake
The impure for the pure?"

"Withered flowers
Fall from the jasmine creeper.
Likewise, O monks,
Let lust and hatred
Fall from you."

— Dhammapada 377

22

Why this Lack of Loving-Kindness ?

Despite the tremendous technological advances of the last few centuries, man is still a beast at heart. Although he is proud of having the latest electronic equipments and enjoying a so-called high standard of living, modern man is not basically different from the Neanderthal man of the Stone Age. We are as aggressively self-centred as were our animalistic ancestors.

Egocentric man is power-hungry, domineering and acquisitive. His great greed for power, position and possessions is truly insatiable. Consequently, this craving (*Tanha*) for more and more has historically been one of the major reasons for colonialism, conflicts and wars in an otherwise peaceful world. Such is man's avariciousness that there is now a growing threat of severe impoverishment in an otherwise rich planet with abundant resources. Man is so selfish that he is sublimely insensitive to the sufferings of others. But if man were free from selfishness, he would be imbued with loving-kindness. For loving-kindness cannot co-exist with selfishness. The two things are mutually exclusive.

Loving-kindness (*Metta*) is usually listed as the first of the four virtues of supreme importance. The virtues of Loving-kindness (*Metta*), Compassion (*Karuna*), Altruistic Joy (*Mudita*) and Equanimity (*Upekkha*) are collectively called the Sublime States (*Brahmavihara*). Sometimes these are termed Boundless States (*Appamanna*). Genuine love is so all-embracing that it operates limitlessly and excludes none.

These four virtues cannot actually be divided into four clear-cut categories for they are all inextricably interlinked. They have many characteristics in common as we shall see. Loving-kindness (*Metta*) is like a thread that connects together the other three virtues. In each of the three virtues there is a strong element of loving-kindness.

It is the total absence of compassion (*Karuna*) in people that makes them very interested in blood sports such as hunting. Those who are truly loving and kind would naturally refrain from all activities that result in the destruction of life such as fishing and slaughtering animals for whatever purpose. Anyone joining the armed forces cannot be unaware that wars necessarily entail the killing of human beings. It is because of their loving-kindness that many vegetarians abstain from eating any creature that has been killed.

It is only when people are lamentably lacking in altruistic joy (*Mudita*) that they are given to bouts of jealousy. Jealousy is a sickly state of mind or attitude wherein one feels uneasy, unhappy or angry because someone has something that one would like very much to have for oneself. This unwholesome state of jealousy operates when a sterile lady gets annoyed with a woman who has just given birth to a baby; when an unsuccessful student, who has failed his exam, starts hating those of his peers who have passed the exam; or, when a man looks angrily at the newly bought car of his neighbour, noticing its superiority over his own old car.

The three instances just mentioned have one thing in common — there is no concern whatsoever for the happiness or welfare of others but only for that of oneself. The non-existence of loving-kindness (*Metta*) is the underlying reason for the prevailing sense of bitterness. Instead of rejoicing in the prosperity of others, these persons are filled with resentment.

The fourth noble virtue, which is termed Equanimity (*Upekkha*) is the state of mental equipoise wherein there is neither attachment to what is pleasurable nor the aversion to what is non-pleasurable. It is an attitude of impartiality.

I have found that the state of loving-kindness, when it exists, is so overpoweringly joyful and even ecstatic at times that both pleasant and non-pleasant thoughts, feelings and sensations somehow seem very unimportant. One is filled with affection that everything else within oneself fades away. The mind remains calm and it is not swayed by praise or blame.

I have also found that whenever the state of loving-kindness is in abeyance the mind gets easily disturbed. Then one's moods change, depending on how one is treated by the outside world. Then one is not immune to flattery, and listening to any kind of strong disapproval of oneself, be it constructive criticism or destructive, can be a very upsetting experience. Besides, one is deeply affected by gain and loss, success and failure as well as pleasure and pain, whereas one remains unaffected by such things when the state of loving-kindness prevails.

Metta (*Maitri* in Sanskrit) is the word for friendship, friendliness, benevolence and goodwill. *Metta* is the strong feeling of deep affection for all living beings, wishing them happiness, good health and prosperity. It is something that is much more than the mere bond of friendship between persons. It is both quantitatively and qualitatively greater than the special bond between mother and child. *Metta*, needless to say, is very different from passionate love that is usually based on physical attraction.

Real affection is rare. Artificial affection is everywhere. More often than not friendships are established in the form of symbiotic relationships, which are noticeable in the animal kingdom when two different creatures live together and depend on each other. But is there *Metta* when relationships are primarily based on mutual support? Out of *Metta* one helps and serves the world without expecting anything in return. *Metta* is that uncommon love that always gives but never asks. Selflessness is the principal characteristic of *Metta*.

How often do we meet people who 'practise *Metta*' with the avowed aim of acquiring merit! They hope to reap the rewards of their loving thoughts and loving deeds either in this life or in the hereafter.

Good works will obviously benefit society. Let us help the needy by all means, bearing in mind the importance of helping others for its own sake. It would be a thousand pities if our practical expressions of *Metta* are vitiated by ulterior motives.

Good thoughts and deeds generate good karma.
Bad thoughts and deeds generate bad karma.

But thoughts and deeds that are devoid of any motive
whatsoever
are karmaless.
Rare indeed are karmaless expressions of love.
Pure indeed are those whose thoughts and deeds are karmaless.

There is a sutta that encapsulates the noble and lofty teachings of the Buddha on the subject of loving-kindness. The verses of the *Mettasutta* are as follows:

1. *"Let him who has attained*
   The tranquil state
   And is skilful in doing good,
   Act as follows:
   He must be capable of being righteous, upright
   And of polite speech,
   Gentle and free from arrogance."

2. *"And be happy and satisfied,*
   Easily supportable,
   Having few problems and worries,
   With calm senses,
   Alert, pride-free
   And greed-free
   When begging for food from homes."

3. *"And he must not behave in a way that is*
   Not morally justifiable,
   Because of which the wise
   Would express their disapproval of him.
   May all creatures be happy and secure!
   May they find happiness!"

4. *"May all beings,*
   Be they weak or strong,
   Be they long, great, medium-sized,
   Short, small or large,"

5. *"Be they seen or unseen,*
   Dwelling near or dwelling far,

Be they born or seeking birth —
May all beings be happy!"

6. *"Let none deceive another!*
   Let none dislike another in any place!
   Out of anger or ill will
   Let none want to harm another!"

7. *"In the same way that a mother*
   At the risk of her own life
   Protects her son, her only son,
   One should have a bountiful
   And limitless mind
   Towards all beings."

8. *"Let him radiate goodwill*
   Or loving-kindness
   To the entire world —
   Above, below and across —
   Without any barriers whatsoever,
   Without any hatred
   And also without any anger."

9. *"Whether he is standing, walking,*
   Sitting or lying down,
   So long as he remains awake,
   He should devote himself
   To radiating loving-kindness.
   This manner of living, they say,
   Is the holiest on earth."

10. *"Not having erroneous views,*
    Being virtuous,
    Having deep insight,
    Having attained detachment from sensuality,
    He never again gets reborn in a mother's womb."

"Let go of anger,
Let go of pride,
Let go of fetters.
In not clinging to name and form

And in calling nothing one's own,
There is freedom from sorrow."

— Dhammapada, 221

The 10 fetters that prevent us from finding Freedom are as follows:

Self-illusion	*Sakkaya – Ditthi*
Doubts	*Vicikiccha*
Indulgence in rites and ceremonies	*Silabbata – Paramasa*
Sense desires	*Kamaraga*
Hatred	*Patigha*
Attachment to Realms of Form	*Ruparaga*
Attachment to Formless Realms	*Aruparaga*
Conceit	*Mana*
Ignorance	*Avijja*

23

Modus Operandi of Meditation

There is a widespread belief that resentments should be forcefully destroyed by using one's will power. Any effort to repress resentments is doomed to failure. Yes, it is certainly possible to brush away *temporarily* anything that is negative in ourselves, but these dark traits, after periods of short-lived inactivity, will start surfacing again, like a temporarily subdued snake that soon coils up and is ready to strike again. That it will certainly do with redoubled strength.

Anyone who tries to use forceful methods or indeed any method for the removal of resentments will only succeed in strengthening his will power, which exists in the form of the 'I'. The resentments are part of the ego, and the ego never wants to be a party to its own destruction. The crafty 'I' will never agree to its own strangulation. Exercising brute force, either grossly or subtly, which people do in the name of 'meditation', does not result in the elimination of the 'I' but only in its reinstatement. Only by the light of intelligence does the 'I' disappear. In the prevailing nothingness there is *Metta*.

Hatred cannot be ironed out by any system, method or technique, but the moment the mind intelligently and fully understands the underlying causes of hatred that had hitherto remained hidden, the mind dissociates itself from hatred. The complex structure of hatred collapses and *Metta* mysteriously appears. In the same way that a roof collapses under the heavy weight of snow, hatred collapses under the weight of intelligence or understanding.

Whenever anger arises, simply stay with it, observe it impartially and just notice its fleeting existence. Watch anger carefully, neither approving nor disapproving of it. Experience anger only mentally, but never express it externally (say, scolding or slapping someone). Watch its operations *within*, and in so doing, see its complex structure and deep origins. Anger would start revealing its ancient roots, provided there is no interference with it whatsoever. Then the once troublesome anger will begin to erode and wear itself out. That will be the beginning of the end of anger. Resentments would, however, occasionally come to the surface. When that happens, once again permit anger to arise and allow it to stay, then it will start telling its last remaining secrets. But once anger finishes relating its story, it would have run out of venom, and then like a slowly moving cloud in the sky, it will pass across the mind. Anger, which in the past was a frequent visitor, will never again want to pay a visit. Eventually, following the purification of the mind, *Metta* will be the norm and not the exception.

Being mentally alert is synonymous with being in a state of wakeful meditation. It is meditation, which is also called awareness, that would clear up man's messy interior. It is a common fallacy to think that *Metta* can be artificially foisted on the mind by various means, especially by the process of repressing anger. Since anger can never coexist with *Metta*, it is first of all necessary to allow the light of awareness to dissolve anger so that the soil of the mind is made ready for the tree of *Metta* to grow and blossom.

Those who realise that it is unsettling, uncomfortable and unhealthy to loathe their enemies, and those who also understand that their simmering hate gnaws away at their peace of mind, which attitude, in turn, leads to sleepless nights, would all of a sudden see a sea change within themselves.

That very seeing, and that very act of changing interiorly, these two things take place at the same time. Seeing intelligently and acting intelligently happen simultaneously. The liberation of the mind from hate occurs when there is this flash of intelligence or clarity, namely the undistorted perception of the existence of hate and all its unpleasant ramifications. In the same way that a withered leaf or a dying branch drops down, our antagonism towards our enemies also drops down. The state of animosity gets automatically replaced by the state of amity, which is *Metta*.

So joyful a state is *Metta* that it precludes the possibility of the existence of any negative state. For instance, the person who is filled with *Metta* is capable of loving even someone who had wronged him in the past. He becomes so forgiving that he can never bear a grudge even against his worst enemies.

> *"We are the products of what we have thought —*
> *We are based on our thoughts,*
> *We are composed of our thoughts.*
> *If one speaks or acts*
> *With a bad thought,*
> *Suffering will follow that person*
> *In the same way that the wheel*
> *Follows the ox's foot that draws the cart."*
>
> — Dhammapada, 1

> *"We are the products of what we have thought —*
> *We are based on our thoughts,*
> *We are composed of our thoughts.*
> *If one speaks or acts*
> *With a pure thought,*
> *Happiness will follow that person*
> *In the same way that the wheel*
> *Follows the ox's foot that draws the cart."*
>
> — Dhammapada, 2

In these very two opening verses of the *Dhammapada* the Buddha shows that man's mind is the sole controller of his destiny in the sense that there is a direct connection between the quality of the thoughts that we think and what will become of us. Although we live in a world with millions of material things around us, the truth is that we live mainly in the private worlds of our minds. Regardless of our external surroundings — be it abject poverty or opulence — our happiness or unhappiness depends respectively on the presence or absence of pure thoughts. Do political, social, economic and other reforms really result in abiding joy and contentment for anyone? It is seldom seen that *changing the mind* is the only means to the creation of a happy world.

> *"In those who have thoughts*
> *Such as 'he insulted me, he hit me,*
> *He subdued me, he stole from me,'*
> *Their anger continues to exist."*
>
> — Dhammapada, 3

> *"In those who have no thoughts*
> *Such as 'he insulted me, he hit me,*
> *He subdued me, he stole from me,'*
> *Their anger has ceased to exist."*
>
> — Dhammapada, 4

> *"Watchfulness is the way to the deathless.*
> *Inattentiveness is the way to death.*
> *The watchful do not die.*
> *The inattentive are like the dead."*
>
> — Dhammapada, 21

> *"By closely understanding this difference,*
> *The wise who are watchful*
> *Rejoice in watchfulness,*
> *And take delight*
> *In the realm of the Pure."*
>
> — Dhammapada, 22

24

Our Enslavement to the Body

'Vijaya' means victory. Why has it become so difficult to win the final victory? This text makes it very clear that the Ultimate cannot be discovered unless our attachment to the body is absolutely abandoned. The short sutta speaks for itself.

The *Vijayasutta* is as follows:

1. *"If while walking, standing,*
   Sitting or lying down,
   A person bends or stretches himself,
   Then his body is in motion."

2. *"This body, which is held together*
   By bones and sinews,
   Which has a plaster of membrane
   And flesh covered with skin,
   Is not seen as it truly is."

3. *"Within it are the intestines,*
   Stomach, lump of the liver,
   Abdomen, heart, lungs,
   Kidneys and spleen."

4. *"Together with mucus,*
   Saliva, sweat, lymph,
   Blood, synovial liquid,
   Bile and fat."

5. *"Always streams of impurities*
Flow forth from
The body's nine openings,
Such as secretions from the eyes and ears."

6. *"From the nose comes mucus,*
And from the mouth
It is sometimes bile
And sometimes phlegm.
Sweat and dirt flow from the body."

7. *"Inside the hollow head*
Is the brain.
The ignorant fool
Regards it as a fine thing."

8. *"The body, when it is dead,*
Becomes bloated
And discoloured.
Discarded in a cemetery,
Relations have no regard for it."

9. *"It is eaten away by dogs,*
Jackals, wolves and worms.
Vultures, crows and other creatures
Consume it."

10. *"Having heard*
And understood the Buddha's words,
The monk sees this body
As it actually is."

11. *"Realising that*
'As is this living body, so is that dead one',
And also understanding that
'This will be like that',
The monk drops his desire for the body,
Both interiorly and exteriorly."

12. *"Such an understanding monk,*
Who is desireless and detached,
Has already found the endless calm,
The unchanging Nirvana."

13. *"This unclean, stinking*
And two-footed body is treasured!
Its filth trickles down
From here and there."

14. *"Having such a body,*
Who would want to praise himself
Or dislike another —-
What else is this
Other than sheer blindness?"

25

The Special Qualities of a Sage (Muni)

To show the so-called high social rank of the Buddha, many misguided devotees refer to him as 'Sakyamuni' — the Noble Sage of the Sakyas. The Buddha is sometimes inappropriately described in this way, as he had descended from the Sakyas, who were a clan of landowners and Kshatriyas (warrior caste) in Kapilavatthu (his birthplace). The clannish designation 'Sakya Sage' is not good enough, nor is it an accurate one for the Buddha's compassion was all-embracing. His universality was without any barriers whatsoever. Here was an extraordinary person whose mind was far beyond the confines of clan or country. It is not by birth that one becomes a Brahmin but solely by the purity of one's thoughts, words and deeds — this is a recurrent theme in many suttas.

One is reminded of those who tried to make a mockery of the message of Jesus by calling him 'King of the Jews' when, in fact, the outlook of Jesus was anything but tribal or racist.

In Buddhist circles the term 'Muni' or 'the Great Sage' refers specifically to the Buddha.

Hindu hermit sages are sometimes referred to as Munis. The word 'muni' has slightly different meanings in other religious traditions. During Rig Vedic times the word included all those who were moved by inner impulses — the enthusiasts, inspired persons and ecstatic mystics. In the later period, at the time of the Brahmanas, 'muni' meant 'sage', 'saint', 'seer', 'ascetic', 'monk', 'devotee' and 'hermit', especially one who has taken the vow of silence.

We know that in ancient Egypt silent men were greatly respected. Silence indicated superiority.

Practising *mauna* (not talking) is comparatively easy. Observe *mauna* if you must, but where is the silence if the mind chatters away all day while the vocal organs remain quiet? The self-induced 'silence' of the lips is not necessarily a sign of the existence of inner silence.

The silence of a great and accomplished Muni is something immensely vaster than the mere abstention from speech. An important characteristic of such a Muni is his *silent mind*. Interestingly, in the *Lalita-Vistara* the word 'Muni' is used to denote an Arhat or a Buddha.

We can learn about the carefree, peaceful and austere lifestyles of monks by turning our attention to the following *Munisutta*:

1. *"Intimate association results in fear.*
   Homelife results in defilement.
   The homeless state,
   The state without associates —
   This is truly the Sage's view."

2. *"Once the ancient growth*
   Has ceased growing,
   He neither replants it
   Nor allows it to arise.
   This lonely wanderer is called a Sage.
   Such a great seer
   Has attained the peaceful state."

3. *"After he considers its causes,*
   And has understood them,
   Craving does not spring up again.
   Such a Sage, seeing the ending
   Of the cycle of births and deaths,
   No longer feels the need to use reason.
   Never again is he reborn."

4. *"He who has understood*
   All the escapist diversions of the mind,

And has no longing for any of them,
Is a Sage.
With graspingness gone
And being free from greed,
His deeds are neither good nor bad,
As he has gone to the other shore."

5. *"Conqueror of all,*
Knowing everything,
Man of great insight
Who is detached from all,
This relinquisher of everything
Whose desires have dropped —-
The wise see him as a Sage."

6. *"Strong in intelligence,*
Virtuous, pure in conduct,
Calm, full of the joy of meditation,
Awake, without ties,
Gentle and cankerless —-
The wise see him as a Sage."

7. *"The Sage walks alone*
And is watchful.
Indifferent to both praise and blame,
Like a lion that is undisturbed by noise,
Like the wind that is not caught in a net,
Like a lotus that is not soiled by water,
He leads others but is never led by them.
The wise regard him as a Sage."

8. *"He is steady,*
As a pillar in a bathing place.
He remains calm
When others speak disparagingly of him.
A passion-free person
Whose sense faculties are composed,
The wise regard him as a Sage."

9. *"Steadfast as a straight shuttle,*
He treats evil deeds
With nothing but disgust,
Having considered what is good and bad.
The wise regard him as a Sage."

10. *"Self-restrained*
And free from wrongdoing,
Being a boy or an adult,
Such a self-restrained one
Neither gets angry nor angers another.
The wise regard him as a Sage."

11. *"Surviving on offerings of food,*
He neither praises nor blames
The donor of alms
When he receives a portion of rice,
Be it from the top, middle or bottom
Of the food container.
The wise see him as a Sage."

The flavour of boiled rice can vary in different parts of the pot used for cooking. Some gourmets like the crusty rice at the bottom.

12. *"The wandering Sage*
Is sexually pure.
Freed from fetters in his earlier years,
He avoids intoxicants
And is devoid of pride.
Being totally liberated,
The wise see him as a Sage."

13. *"Having seen through the world,*
He sees the Truth.
Having crossed the sea of existence,
With all his bonds broken,
Being unblemished,
The wise see him as a Sage."

14. *"The two of them*
Have quite different lifestyles

And different dwelling places —
The householder and his wife on the one hand,
And the selfless virtuous person on the other.
The unrestrained householder
Is given to the killing of living creatures,
Whereas the restrained Sage
Always protects them."

15. *"When they fly in the sky,*
A crested peacock with a blue neck
Cannot equal the speed of a swan.
In the same way, a householder
Can never equal a monk —
The solitary Sage
Who meditates in the forest."

26

Short Sutta on Sincere Friendship

Hirisutta

1. *"He who oversteps modesty*
   And feels contempt for it,
   Who declares his friendship,
   Saying 'I am a friend',
   But avoids doing what can be done,
   One should regard such a person as 'not my friend'."

2. *"He who uses pleasant words*
   When conversing with friends,
   But fails to take action,
   The wise take a dim view of him,
   Seeing him not so much a doer as a mere talker."

3. *"He is not a friend*
   Who is eagerly suspicious and faultfinding.
   But the person with whom one can securely stay,
   Like a son resting at his mother's breast,
   Is an inseparable friend indeed."

4. *"While carrying his human burden,*
   He reaps the fruit of his deeds
   Wherein there is joy and the happiness
   That is praiseworthy."

5. *"Tasting the sweetness*
   Of solitude and silence,

He is free from fear
And without any blemish.
In the Dharma he finds bliss."

Who then is a true friend? The definition of a true friend is wholly *subjective*.

While hurrying along the road, a kindly old lady sees an emaciated hungry beggar standing on the pavement. The sight of his misery moves her profoundly. She presents the starving man with a square meal. Thereafter the beggar thankfully regards her as his true friend.

A teenage girl, who loves to hitchhike, stands at the side of a road and holds high her thumb. Scorched by the hot sun, she waits for several hours but no motorist offers her a lift. The tired girl grows impatient. At last a lorry driver stops his vehicle and offers her a free ride. The grateful girl thereafter views the man she has just met as her true friend.

A chronic alcoholic ends up out of pocket. He wants very much to have another drink but realises that he has no more money left. A down-and-out in the same city takes pity on him and offers him a beer in a nearby pub. The alcoholic is so pleased that he starts regarding the down-and-out as his only true friend!

From the Buddhist standpoint, a true friend is someone who is compassionate and thoughtful enough not only to introduce people to the Dharma with all its treasures, but also to explain the sublime teachings at great length. He is never tired of talking to one and all about the Buddha and his message. He does so out of compassion, without any pecuniary motive whatsoever. Ours is such a degenerate world that false friends are aplenty, whereas sincere friends with a loving and caring disposition are so few. Real friends are very rare and almost impossible to discover. There are people who go off in search of real friends. After a lifetime of searching they give up trying to find perfect companions. Then the sad truth dawns on them that finding a genuine friend is as difficult as meeting an angel in a street.

The so-called friendships that we strike up in the modern world are mostly based on the principle of mutual help and mutual support. People like to form friendships because of the realisation that their closeness and interdependence will be mutually beneficial either in the present or future. For example, when someone is worried and in great distress, we give the advice and the comfort that the unfortunate person badly needs, but we do so only because of our unexpressed expectation that our 'loving care' would someday be reciprocated by the recipient of our 'good' intentions. Nearly always we expect a reward for our 'services' and 'good' deeds either in this life or in the hereafter. A true friend, in contrast, offers his heartfelt help with no strings attached. Neither does he expect any material benefit in return for his good deeds nor does he derive any psychological satisfaction by doing them. For he never tells himself, "I am virtuous" or "I am a good fellow". There is in him an attitude of *total detachment* when he helps others. He is not at all interested in the question of acquiring merit by performing meritorious deeds. Such is his motivelessness and purity that there is no creation of karma.

When a man is too much of a snob he would tend to cultivate the rich and the famous. By the same token, he would tend to neglect and forget former friends who are now in dire poverty. A faithful friend would never desert you when you are in reduced circumstances. On the contrary, a loyal being becomes even more attentive to his friend's needs in times of adversity.

In the name of friendship, promiscuous men are given to flattering women, which involves praising passionately, among other things, their beauty and charms. By feeding womanly vanity, and by pandering to the egos of females, these pleasure seekers manage to bed them. After a time these opportunists lose interest in their partners. Next they abandon the women to whom they had once professed their undying love. When they thus leave their lovers, after having broken their hearts, these fleeting friendships end in bitterness, tears and suffering.

A true friend never shirks from criticising and complaining whenever it becomes necessary to do so. This means that he does not mind courting unpopularity and disapproval because he realises that constructive criticism cannot but bring lasting benefits to those who have gone astray. Whenever he has to make a correction, a true friend never bears any malice, although at times his comments might seem like uncaring remarks. A true friend's corrective words might temporarily hurt one's feelings, yet they will heal many an inner illness over the long term. Must we not therefore be grateful to friends, regardless of whether they are benign or malign, who take the trouble to criticise us, especially when they bring to our attention the various prejudices that lurk in the remote regions of our minds? The truth of the matter is that we deeply dislike friends who are critical of us. Is it not true that others' criticisms often mirror our hidden impurities or imperfections?

The lack of true friends is one of the major causes of unhappiness in society. Who likes to be unloved? Then out of the depths of despair, one starts telling oneself, "is it fair to blame the outside world for our unpleasant state of friendlessness? Must I not blame myself for my painful situation? I am only reaping the bitter fruits of my own past misdeeds, in other words, my karma."

That is how one reacts at first, but on further reflection, one begins to have a new approach to the problem, which is as follows.

We can surely ask ourselves several questions: Why this pathological craving for friends? Every form of craving is a manifestation of *Tanha*, which means thirst or craving. Craving, we know, is not only the main cause of suffering but also the major factor in the continuation of our sorrowful cycle of rebirths. Should we not therefore discover for ourselves that state of absolute self-reliance and total independence, wherein at all times the mind is no longer attached to *anything* or *anyone*? Why then the need for friends, even true ones?

27

The Shore Beyond Samsarā

Once the Buddha was staying on a stone seat in the realm of a demon called the Yakkha Sukiloma. When the Yakkha Sukiloma and another demon by the name of the Yakkha Khara were going past the Buddha, the yakkhas started talking to each other. Let us consider the *Sukilomasutta.*

Khara:	"That person is a recluse."
Sukiloma:	"No, he is not a recluse! He is a contemptible ascetic. Yet I will make sure whether he is a recluse or a contemptible ascetic."

Sukiloma next went towards the Buddha and pressed his body against that of the Master, who then turned away.

Sukiloma:	"Recluse, are you fearful of me?"
The Buddha:	*"Friend, I am not afraid of you* *But your touch is evil."*
Sukiloma:	"Recluse, I will ask you a question. If you fail to answer it I will either break up your mind, or split your heart, or grab you by the feet and throw you right over the Ganges to the other bank of the river."
The Buddha:	*"But, O friend,* *I don't see anybody in this world,*

Including the worlds of the Devas, Maras, Brahmans,
Nor among the recluses and Brahmins
As well as gods and men,
Who is capable of breaking up my mind,
Splitting my heart,
Grabbing my feet
And throwing me over the Ganges
To the other bank of the river.
In spite of that,
O friend, ask me what you wish."

Sukiloma: "What is the origin of passion, hate, aversion, delight and horror? How do they come into existence? What is the source of the doubts that trouble the mind in the same way that boys annoy a crow?"

The Buddha: *"Passion and hate*
Have their origin in the body.
Aversion, delight and horror
Spring from this body.
Like boys that annoy a crow,
The doubts that trouble the mind
Come into being from this body."

"They grow out of craving,
They come out of the self,
Like the tender shoots of the banyan tree.
They are related
To the pleasures of the senses,
Like the maluva creeper
That spreads over the woods."

"They who understand from where it comes,
Are no longer involved in it.
O Yakkha, please listen to me.
They cross this stream
That is not easy to cross,

Which until now has not been crossed.
They do not get reborn."

It is a total fallacy that we are born only once. Many persons believe that there is only one single lifetime. They do not realise that some of their traits or latent tendencies have been carried over by them from their previous existences to their present one. Such short-sightedness results in a certain light-hearted and superficial attitude to life. Instead of delving deeply into these latent tendencies, which if correctly understood will invariably result in their dissolution, people waste their present life by engaging themselves in useless activities, especially merry-making and dissipating their energies in the pursuit of pleasure. They fail to see that every pleasure is short-lived, and leads inevitably to sorrow. No pleasure is of everlasting duration. Addicted to the pleasures of the senses, we foolishly prolong our samsaric sojourn.

Man's wretched round of seemingly endless births and deaths becomes truly a state of 'perpetual wandering'. This is the stream that we have to cross, the sea of life — *samsara*.

Philosophically speaking, *samsara* is also the continual formation and re-formation of our psychological traits; it is the constantly changing combinations of our tendencies. At this moment in time the illusory 'I', which exists but precariously, is the combination of certain specific traits. The next moment the chameleon-like crafty 'I' has suddenly become the temporary gathering together of a different set of traits. Some of the stronger traits are difficult to drop with the result that they re-form in different combinations and emerge from life to life.

In Hindu thought the term *samsara* refers to transmigratory existence. It is the passage of the soul from one body into another body at death. Every new life is an episode in a sorrowful series of painful births, deaths and rebirths. The body dies and disintegrates but the deathless soul moves from the old body to the new. This plausible theory is based on the assumption that a soul in the form of an immutable entity actually exists. But does it?

Let us leave aside for a moment this theory. By understanding the importance of constant alertness and vigilance, and by seeing the mind's escapist fondness for metaphysical speculation, we can no longer avoid facing reality. Let us be perfectly honest when posing the question — does the soul really exist?

Within this constantly changing psycho-physical organism of ours, is there anything that has the attribute of permanency? Within it, is there anything that is not subject to change, decay and death? I for one would much like to see, feel and touch this so-called soul. The belief in an eternal soul or 'self' is nothing but a mere invention of the mind. This very comforting concept of the soul was one of man's cleverest inventions, as it provided him with a way of deluding himself into believing that there is a hidden something abiding somewhere that is indestructible.

This grandiose product of our distorted imagination springs from our craving for a haven of security, for ours is a situation wherein everything within ourselves — thoughts, feelings and sensations, indeed our very cells — are all in a state of change, movement, transitoriness and absolute insecurity. The belief in a soul gives us a sense of stability and security. Besides, by believing in the existence of a soul, we can subtly confer on ourselves both spiritual honours and religious respectability. How we like to flatter ourselves by thinking that we have some vague divine spark or soul which, according to the theologians, makes man superior to animals, thereby investing us with the right to hunt, maim and kill animals! We justify cruelty to animals on the grounds that these poor creatures have no souls! How we like to think that we are somehow special because we have souls, whereas in truth we are only temporary collections! We are mere bundles of beliefs, thoughts, traits, tendencies and the like, all of which are changeable at any moment.

When, and how, did the cycle of *samsara* begin? Why did it start? Philosophers can ponder over these mentally stimulating questions. They can ceaselessly speculate about the whys and wherefores for many lives and still be in the dark. Paradoxically, some might find enjoyment and pleasure in the process of straining their brains while searching for the right answers. They can certainly think very deeply about these matters till they are blue in the face.

Don't these questions, despite their seeming importance, fall into the category of spiritual imponderables?

Supposing someone should discover the origin of *samsara*, would that discovery be of any assistance in attaining Enlightenment? Evidently, it is not necessary to have such knowledge in the sense that it is not a prerequisite for *Nirvana*.

According to the Samyutta Nikaya,

> *"This samsara is without discoverable beginning."*
> — *The Connected Discourses of the Buddha* vol.2 p.1694

The above-mentioned statement of the Venerable Sariputta was later repeated verbatim by the Buddha.

Extricating ourselves from samsaric suffering is far more important and urgent than knowing about its beginning.

> *"O monk,*
> *Empty the boat!*
> *When emptied,*
> *It will move fast.*
> *Being freed from the bonds*
> *Of lust and hatred,*
> *You will go*
> *To Nirvana."*
>
> — Dhammapada, 369

28

Monks Must Lead Pure Lives

Purity is the theme in the following sutta, which is called *Dhammakariyasutta* or *Kapilasutta*.

1. *"Living righteously*
   And leading the holy life,
   This is the best gem,
   If anyone leaves hearth and home
   For the state of homelessness."

2. *"But if he uses bad language,*
   Gets pleasure from being cruel,
   If he is beastly and wicked,
   Such a person adds to his own impurity."

3. *"The monk who loves to argue angrily,*
   And is shrouded in delusion,
   Fails to understand the Dharma
   That the Buddha taught."

4. *"Damaging his own developed mind,*
   Overpowered by ignorance,
   He does not know that defilement
   Is the way to hell."

5. *"Having now entered*
   A place of suffering,
   Moving from womb to womb,

Going from darkness to darkness,
Such a monk truly finds himself
In a state of misery
After his life has ended."

6. *"A cess-pit that has not been cleaned for years*
Is overflowing with excrement.
In the same way,
It would be difficult to purify someone
Who has sunk
Into the depths of depravity."

7. *"Monks, if you come across such a monk*
With a craving for home,
Having evil intentions and evil thoughts
As well as doing evil deeds,"

8. *"With one accord keep away from him.*
Cast him aside
As if he were sweepings.
Discard him
As if he were rubbish."

9. *"Then, as one sifts*
The grain from the chaff,
Remove those
Who only regard themselves as recluses
But are not real ones.
Get rid of those
With evil intentions and evil actions."

10. *"Not only be pure*
But live with those that are pure,
Being alert and attentive.
Then, being harmonious and wise,
Your suffering will be at an end."

Every monk is obliged to observe strictly the rules of the *Vinaya*, which are carefully laid down in the *Vinaya Pitaka*. These disciplinary rules that monks must follow constitute the third part of the *Tripitaka*. Here one can find in detail the regulations relating to the moral, ethical and religious aspects of the lives of monks. So important are these rules that there is a special school of Buddhism in East Asia called the Vinaya School.

A monk's renunciatory ceremony includes, among other deeds, the declaration of the three jewels — "I take refuge in the Buddha, I take refuge in the Dharma, I take refuge in the Sangha" and the promise to observe the precepts. Admission to the Sangha is called *Pabajja* or 'leaving the world'. Needless to say, 'leaving the world' cannot be put into effect unless the monk leaves behind all the things of the world — family, wealth, sensual enjoyments, politics and the like. We shall later discuss the question of whether or not it is right and proper for monks to go into politics.

The Sangha is the term that is commonly used when referring to the community of Buddhist monks. The simple and pious lay folk, who innocently provide the Sangha with food, medicines and the like, often fail to see the grim facts behind a monk's façade of holiness. Awe-struck by the sight of the saffron-coloured robe, they rarely know the hidden character of the wearer of the robe whom they serve with great devotion. However, should the generous food donors discover a bad monk within a community of good monks, they often tend to lump the false monk and the true monks together. Consequently, one black sheep within the Sangha can sometimes bring the entire Sangha into disrepute.

The ultimate sanction that genuine monks have is to expel bogus monks from their order. The monks who refuse to respect the *Vinaya* rules can be thus ostracised by the Sangha. The laypersons on their part can withhold the provision of alms to monks who are guilty of misconduct. The laypersons can continue imposing these sanctions until the bad monks mend their ways.

If a monk feels that he cannot abide by the *Vinaya* rules and thereby undergo rigorous hardships, he is at liberty to leave the order. In Sri Lanka a strong stigma is attached to the abandonment of the order. A renunciant who renounces the order is regarded as regressive. But in Thailand many boys and men become ordained monks for limited periods, and there are others who keep their vows for an entire lifetime. Many Thais think that being a monk is a good discipline even for a short time. Some schoolboys become monks for a few weeks, often when they are on vacation. A Sri Lankan monk once expressed his disapproval when I told him about the Thai practice of short-term monkhood. "A man who abandons the world and becomes a monk has no more connection with the world," he argued. He added, "becoming a monk is the act of throwing away the world with all its attractions into the rubbish bin. Afterwards how can you possibly have any liking for what you have discarded forever into the rubbish bin?"

Renunciation necessarily implies losing interest in all things mundane — property and wealth, sex, marriage and family. But if a monk retains any interest in them, that is a sure sign that he is not a real renunciant.

A bogus monk would sport a shaved head, put on an ochre robe and make a parade of his asceticism.

I have met several Buddhist monks who, alas, had no qualms about indulging in sex, and in this manner violate one of the basic moral precepts 'I will abstain from sexual misconduct.'

I have also known money-making monks. They have become the managers of institutions as they prefer administration to meditation. They have unfortunately succumbed to the temptation to become persons of importance in society, once again forgetting the fact that they have given up society with all its charms. Only in theory have they renounced society. A monk's begging bowl is surely a constant reminder that he has chosen the austere life of poverty and insecurity. Therefore any activity that is related to the world of finance should always be an anathema. Ramakrishna Paramahamsa's great aversion to gold, silver and coins was such that he could not even touch them. Renunciation was second nature to this Hindu saint.

Everyday in society there are thousands of financial transactions. Millions handle money. Therefore cash and coins must be viewed as unclean things. A monk who has any contact with money inevitably contaminates himself both physically and morally.

If Buddhist monks were one-hundred-percent otherworldly in

their outlook and conduct, as they surely should be, politics would have no place whatsoever in their lives. Yet it is alarming and indeed surprising that some unwise 'renunciants' have not only entered the political arena but also become parliamentarians. O tempora, O mores! Is there anything more worldly than engaging oneself in politics?

What is really behind the professed policies of political parties? What are the unpleasant facts that lie behind the camouflage of their high-sounding idealism and plans for social betterment? Politicians are mostly interested in the acquisition of power, position and prestige. Pecuniary self-interest is often the motivation for their 'altruistic' deeds. In the light of these truths, can we think highly of monks who enter politics and inevitably get drawn into these self-centred pursuits of politicians? When the once unknown monk turned politician wins some fame, he will get a swollen head, thus greatly strengthening his ego. When the once poverty-stricken monk yields to the temptation to accept bribes, he would soon have a tidy fortune. Before long the monk's professed quest for *Nirvana* will have to be postponed indefinitely, if not abandoned altogether.

Politicians concern themselves mostly with capturing political power by hook or by crook. Since politics has become the domain of crooks (what a far cry from the concept of philosopher kings suggested in Plato's 'The Republic!'), honest and conscientious citizens as a rule avoid politics like the plague. Persons with high moral standards find it difficult to endure the machinations of politicians. Politicians have to spend much time and energy working out various strategies for gaining power, and retaining it thereafter. That is for them an important part of their daily lives, but such a demeaning preoccupation would be unbecoming to a Buddhist monk. Instead of regarding his political opponents as his arch-enemies, it would be far better for a monk, if he is involved in politics, to adopt a neutral attitude towards it. But an attitude of *total indifference* to, and *non-involvement* in, politics is the best, which course would make it considerably easier for him to radiate compassion (*Karuna*) to one and all.

Politicians are given to arguing excessively, quarrelling with each other and shouting their opponents down during debates. The gift of the gab is a very useful asset to any politician. A monk, however, who emulates Buddhist saints, would only talk a little. The Buddha's foremost disciple, Sariputta, spoke in moderation. Silence was a noteworthy characteristic of the Enlightened ones. A taciturn monk will probably fare badly if he ever enters politics.

If a monk wants to keep calm (*Samatha*), he would have been well advised to keep away from the hurly-burly of legislative assemblies. The cut and thrust of politics will strike a discordant note. In the heat of an argument a political Bhikkhu might lose his temper, especially if his political opponents start making false accusations against him. If the monk finds himself filled with anger (*Dosa*), will he be a credit to the community of Buddhist monks (*Sangha*)?

For more than a decade I worked for Parliament House in South Australia. My work involved providing parliamentarians with information. It was an interesting period when I discovered the hidden problems of politicians that the public hardly knows. On one occasion a lady parliamentarian, who was suffering from depression, came to me and made a confession. She said, "I can't survive in the world of politics without having to tell lies. We're professional liars! If I'm caught lying I feel embarrassed. Then I try to cover up the lie by telling more lies! In public life, you see, we have to fight to safeguard our reputations." Now, for all practical purposes, a political monk who is given to lying (*Musavada*), and who tries to safeguard his reputation in this way would be striving to protect, strengthen and prolong the existence of his ego — the very obstacle that gets in the way of his Illumination.

Ignoring the fact that ambition in any form falls into the category of craving (*Tanha*), ambitious monks argue that they had over the centuries been advisers to various kings and ministers. These monks try to carve out for themselves careers in parliamentary politics, perhaps by playing advisory roles. If that is all they want to do, this can be quietly done from the monasteries where they reside, without becoming the members of any parliament. How they try to justify their ambitions by maintaining that they are the rightful protectors and guardians of the Dharma!

Truth is invincible. The Dharma can never be defeated or destroyed by its enemies. The Dharma has its own inherent strength. The Dharma is capable of successfully defending itself against all dangers. Does the Dharma really need the protection of any outside agency? Do we need the 'help' or 'services' of political monks to 'save' the Dharma? The question is whether or not these ambitious and mentally troubled monks have the requisite purity and insight to understand the Dharma correctly, and thereby use the Dharma for the purpose of saving *themselves* from the burden of their past karma.

Expressed differently, none need worry about saving the Dharma from destruction. But applying the Dharma to save ourselves should be our sole concern.

The best thing that monks can do now is to continue doing what they have been doing so well for centuries — the study and exposition of the Buddhist scriptures for the benefit of the laity. That has historically been their speciality. They should stick to it, for politics is the exclusive realm of Mammon.

In his penetrating work on statecraft titled 'The Prince', Niccolo Machiavelli advocated the use of cunning means for the achievement of one's political aims. A prince, for example, must *appear* to be compassionate and *make an impression* of being a man of good faith and integrity. Above all, he should *pretend* to be religious, which is a very important attribute of any ruler who is determined to be successful in his field. Does this mean that the Machiavellian monks of the future will only have the façade of piety while being vile?

Satiated after eating, lions like to rest for a few days. The monk Santakaya's behaviour was closely akin to that of a lion. He had in fact been one in a previous existence. Steady and slow in his movements, Santakaya was usually quiet and untroubled. Some monks reported the matter to the Buddha, who remarked that monks must be calm and composed in the manner of Santakaya.

"The monk who is calm in body,
Speech and mind,
Who maintains his composure,
Who has thrown away
The things of this world,
Is truly a peaceful person."

— Dhammapada, 378

29

Why this Senseless Sacrificial Slaughter of Cows ?

The spirit of sacrifice expresses itself in manifold ways. In theistic religions it is the practice to make offerings to the Divine or to a deity from the animal or vegetable kingdoms. Often offerings of food, drink, perfume, incense and the like are made. Sometimes precious articles in gold and silver are offered. Objects placed on altars can be regarded as sacrifices, provided they are expressions of thanksgiving or atonement for wrongdoings. In the Christian tradition there is the strange belief that Jesus, by means of the crucifixion, offered himself to God in order to save man, as though salvation can be experienced vicariously! Sacrifice can also mean the giving up of something bad (such as drug addiction) or something pleasant (such as sexual indulgence) for the sake of achieving some higher spiritual objective.

"If any devotee offers Me with *love and devotion* a leaf, a flower or water," declared Lord Krishna in the *Bhagavad Gita*, "I will accept it." It is implied that any offering, which is devoid of love and devotion, will be unacceptable. Love and devotion, in other words, are the two essential requirements that the Lord expects. Apparently the Lord craves for love! If He grants His favours only to those who sing His praises and shower Him with affectionate offerings, and if the Lord frowns on those who are lacking in such devotion, it only shows that God, if He exists at all, is certainly *not* 'all-loving'. He is also, evidently, a being with human traits, who is full of predilections and aversions, like anyone who is entangled in *Samsara*.

Because Buddhists do not believe in the existence of a God, but rather regard this concept as nothing but a clever creation of man's imagination, on the whole they see the utter absurdity of making sacrifices to the Divine. However, it has long been the practice in Sri Lanka, on account of the powerful influence of Hinduism on Buddhist society, for many Buddhists to make sacrifices to deities. Next they request the deities to do them various favours.

When a person has a profound understanding of the great truth that 'one is one's own liberator' (*Atta hi attano natho*), his independent and self-reliant outlook is such that he realises the meaninglessness of trying to appease celestial beings with the intention of persuading them to do him favours. Admittedly, celestial beings, such as devas, can do us minor favours, but it is doubtful if they can make ineffective the operations of the karmic law in certain situations. If a man is guilty of murder, has any celestial being the power to nullify the consequences of that terrible crime? By the same token, can any deva help us to cleanse away our defilements such as hate (*Dosa*), greed (*Lobha*) or pride (*Mana*)? It is easy to overlook the fact that many invisible creatures have yet to drop their defilements. These unseen beings are, fundamentally, not different from ourselves, which explains why they, like ourselves, continue to remain 'perpetual wanderers' in the sea of life (*Samsara*).

In Hindu thought, letting go or detachment (*Tyaga*) is the essence of karma yoga, which is detachment from the fruits of one's thoughts, words and deeds. Expressed differently, it is the renunciation of the desire for any reward whatsoever for all one's sacrificial offerings. This is, at best, only an ideal, because in practice there is hardly any sense of detachment when Hindus give offerings to their numerous deities.

It is invariably the case that when a Hindu offers, say, a tray of flowers and fruits to a deity as a sacrifice, there is deep down in his heart of hearts this expectation — "please god, this is just a little something for you in the hope that you would in exchange do me the following favour ... (such as) help my son to find himself a good bride with a big dowry, or help my husband to find a better job, or help my son to pass his exam." Rarely, if ever, does he make an offering out of pure love, for every offering serves some ulterior purpose.

If the devotee were imbued with pure love he would love God for His own sake and never ask for help. It is probably a shortcoming on God's part that He looks with favour on those who make sacrifices. If God were imbued with pure love, would He not go to the aid of all, whether or not sacrifices are made?

One wonders how some so-called Buddhists ever bring themselves to make sacrifices, which are usually made at Hindu shrines. An intelligent Buddhist is a person who understands the operations of the law of karma. He knows that he alone is in control of his destiny. He sees that his present sufferings, which are the inevitable outcome of his past demeritorious deeds, words and thoughts, cannot be totally prevented by means of sacrifices. Similarly, he realises that someday in the future he will have to reap the fruits of what he is sowing now — his present thoughts, words and actions.

What, if any, are the sacrifices that a Buddhist needs doing? On the altar of purity he can ensure the termination of all his taints. He can, for instance, sacrifice greed (*Lobha*), hatred (*Dosa*) and delusion (*Moha*).

In the *Brahmanadhammikasutta* the Buddha denounced the degenerate Brahmins, who persuaded the king to do the terrible deed of slaying cows at sacrifices.

Many wealthy and elderly Kosalan Brahmins called on the Buddha. At that time he was staying at Savatthi in Jeta's grove in the park of Anathapindika. After exchanging greetings with the Master, these decrepit Brahmins sat down by his side, and posed an interesting question: "O Venerable Gotama, do the present-day Brahmins conform to the Brahman-Dharma or customs of the ancient Brahmins?"

> *"The present-day Brahmins,"* replied the Buddha,
> *"Do not appear to be conforming*
> *To the Brahman-Dharma*
> *Of the ancient Brahmins."*

"Provided we are not causing an inconvenience," they said, "let the Venerable Gotama explain to us the customs of the ancient ones."

> *"Then listen attentively,"* said the Buddha,
> *"To what I am going to say."*

1. *"The sages of yesteryear*
Were well-behaved and austere.
The objects of their five sense organs
Having fallen away,
They devoted themselves
To their own spiritual good."

2. *"Those Brahmins owned*
Neither cattle, gold nor corn.
Their riches consisted in the corn
Of meditation.
Leading the holy life
Was their treasure."

3. *"The food was prepared for them*
And placed outside doors.
This they regarded
As offerings of faith
To seekers."

4. *"Prosperous persons from afar*
Worshipped those Brahmins
And showed reverence for them
With differently coloured clothes, beds and homes."

5. *"The Brahmins were inviolate*
And invincible.
The Dharma was their protection.
None would close his door
On a Brahmin."

6. *"They from youth to forty-eight*
Were chaste and celibate.
In former times they were devoted
To knowledge and the holy life."

7. *"Brahmins did not wed women*
Of other castes
Nor did they buy brides.
By common consent they lived together,
Linked by bonds of love."

8. *"Brahmins did not have sexual intercourse,*
Except at the end of menstruation."

9. *"They valued purity and virtue,*
Correctness, gentleness, austerity,
Tenderness, compassion and patience."

10. *"The best of them — the highest Brahmin —*
Would not indulge in sexual intercourse
Even while dreaming."

11. *"Emulating him,*
The wise of this world
Extol purity,
Virtue and patience."

12. *"After requesting rice, beds, clothes,*
Ghee and oil,
And having properly brought them together,
They made their sacrifices.
These sacrifices did not involve
The slaughter of cows."

13. *"Just like our mother,*
Father, brother, or other relations,
The cows are our best friends
Who bring forth medicines."

14. *"They provide food,*
They provide strength,
Similarly they give us
A good complexion and happiness.
Seeing the truth of this,
No cows were killed."

15. *"Tender, large-bodied,*
Beautiful and famous,
The Brahmins had their own
High standards of right and wrong.
They prospered
For the duration of their lives on earth."

16. *"But then they changed.*
Little by little, they noticed
The king's majesty
And ornamented women."

17. *"Well-constructed carriages*
Drawn by thoroughbreds,
Coloured carpets,
Partitioned palaces and houses,"

18. *"The vast wealth of people,*
Herds of cows
And fair females —
All these the Brahmins eagerly desired."

19. *"With this as their objective,*
They composed hymns
And visited Okkaka and said,
'King, you have much wealth and corn.
Sacrifice, for vast is your property!
Sacrifice, for vast is your wealth!'"

20. *"Thereupon the king,*
The lord of the warriors,
Who was persuaded by the Brahmins,
Performed these sacrifices —
Assamedha (sacrifice of horse),
Purisamedha (sacrifice of man),
Sammapasa (probably it means animal sacrifice)
And Vajapeyya (drink of strength or of battle).
After offering the sacrifices,
He gave wealth to the Brahmins —"

21. *"Cows, beds, clothes, ornamented women,*
Well-constructed carriages drawn by thoroughbreds,
Coloured carpets,"

22. *"Beautiful and partitioned palaces*
That were filled with corn.
This wealth he gave to the Brahmins."

23. *"After receiving this wealth,*
They hoarded it.
They wanted more of it.
Their craving for wealth began to grow.
With this as their objective,
They composed hymns
And visited Okkaka again and said,"

24. *"Just as water, earth, gold, wealth and corn,*
So are cows for men,
For this is needed for human beings.
Sacrifice, for vast is your property!
Sacrifice, for vast is your wealth!"

25. *"Thereupon the king,*
The lord of the warriors,
Who was persuaded by the Brahmins,
Had many hundreds of thousands
Of cows slain as a sacrifice."

26. *"Neither by means of their feet*
Nor by means of their horns
Do cows harm anyone in any way.
With goat-like tenderness
Cows yield pails of milk,
Yet the king, holding them by the horns,
Had them slain."

27. *"When the cows were*
Being killed for the sacrifice,
'This is wrong!' cried out the gods,
The fathers, Indra,
The Asuras and demons."

28. *"In former times*
There were three diseases —
Desire, hunger and decay.
Now with the killing of cattle
The number has risen
To ninety-eight!"

29. *"This injustice of violence*
Is of ancient origin.
Innocent cows are killed.
The sacrificing priests
Have deviated from justice."

30. *"The wise denounce*
This ancient and inferior practice.
When people notice it,
They blame the sacrificing priest."

31. *"When justice disappeared in this way,*
The workers (Sudras)
Clashed with the traders (Vaisyas),
And the Kshatriyas (lawmakers, law enforcers and military)
Disagreed in many ways,
And the wife had scorn for her husband."

32. *"The Kshatriyas and the Brahmins,*
And the others who had hitherto been
Separated by their castes,
Were overpowered by
Sensual pleasures."

The wealthy Brahmins exclaimed, "Excellent, O Venerable Gotama, it is excellent! Just as one moves to an upright position what has been overthrown, or divulges what had remained a secret, or gives directions to a person who has become lost, or is an oil lamp and a light to those in the dark, so has the Venerable Gotama illustrated the Dharma in many ways. We take refuge in the Buddha, the Dharma and the Sangha. May the Venerable Gotama accept us as his followers, we who have taken refuge in him until the end of our days."

30

Use a Strong Boat for Sailing Through

The *Navasutta* is a short discourse on the importance of selecting a learned and trustworthy teacher, who is not only morally good but also correct in his understanding of the Dharma.

1. *"A man must honour him*
   From whom he learns the Dharma.
   One should do this
   Just as the deities honour Indra.
   When a person of much learning
   Is thus honoured, he is pleased,
   And he makes others aware of the Dharma."

2. *"The wise man*
   Who associates with such a learned teacher,
   Attentively listens to him,
   And takes action
   In accordance with the Dharma.
   He thus becomes a learned
   And intelligent person himself."

3. *"But when one serves*
   A low and foolish person,
   Who has not understood the meaning of the Dharma
   And is given to envy,
   Then one approaches one's death
   Without comprehending the Dharma clearly,
   Being troubled by doubts about it."

4. *"Like a man who is swept along*
On the tide of a swollen and swiftly flowing river,
Will he be capable of assisting others
To cross it?"

5. *"In the same way, how can a man,*
Who has not clearly understood the Dharma,
Who pays no heed to the words of the learned,
Who himself is lacking in understanding
And is still having doubts,
Be capable of enlightening others?"

6. *"As one who goes on board a strong boat,*
Equipped with oar and rudder,
Knowing how to handle it,
And being skilful and alert,
So in the boat
He will carry across many."

7. *"In the same manner,*
The one who has knowledge
And is advanced,
Who is learned and fearless,
Having understood it himself,
Could be instrumental
In making others see it themselves,
Provided they are capable
Of listening attentively."

8. *"Therefore, one must associate*
With a pious person
Who is both intelligent
And erudite.
By understanding the meaning,
By going along the path that he points out,
And by completely grasping the Dharma,
One finds happiness."

The Buddhist concept of the guru, as evidenced by statements in this *sutta*, is to some extent different from the Hindu one.

Hindu gurus, like their Buddhist counterparts, are also guides and teachers but the former are increasingly becoming cult leaders in the modern world. Hindu gurus claim to be revealers of the Truth. They have traditionally played a leading role in society by being responsible for the spiritual and moral illumination of people. Gurus are seen as rays of light in a world enmeshed in the darkness of materialism. Many gurus have claimed to be Jagadgurus or World Teachers, representatives of the Divine, if not God Himself. But when a guru's character falls short of society's expectations, he usually tries to rationalise his behaviour by saying that the world must uncomplainingly accept his shortcomings in the same way that devotees accept God, who is also full of contradictions and imperfections.

By and large, Buddhists remain unaffected by those who conceitedly claim to be agents of the Absolute, for they know that final Freedom from suffering cannot be found through the agency of another. They are also aware deep down that they alone are personally and self-reliantly responsible for the eventual elimination of all their inner impurities. Why waste your precious time and energy by seeking the services of gurus, priests or any intermediaries whatsoever?

In no sense is a learned Buddhist teacher a manifestation of the Buddha. But a Hindu guru, according to the tantrics, is the earthly manifestation of the Supreme Guru, who enters into the earthly guru when a pupil is being initiated by him. That is the moment when the pupil is given a sacred mantra that will supposedly guide him throughout his life. In ancient times the pupil would live with his guru for about a dozen years, studying the Vedas at the feet of his master, caring for his mentor's cattle and doing his agricultural duties. He lived with the guru and had to show total obedience and respect to him. In the Buddhist tradition, by contrast, the pupil is not bound by such requirements. There might arise a bond of friendship between the pupil and the learned Buddhist teacher. Between them there is simply a bond of affection and the pupil is not kept in bondage to the master.

One meets pundits on Buddhism who are exceptionally well

versed in the scriptures but unfortunately a good many of them have no morals. They seem to think that it is enough to have a mere intellectual understanding of the Dharma. Such learned men are like lovely jasmine flowers that have no perfume. It is often difficult to tell whether or not a monk is a highly moral man. This can cause difficulty when searching for a suitable teacher.

When seeking a guru, it is very rare, if ever, that seekers end up finding a suitable and sincere seer. This is partly because the world abounds in false prophets. In their long search for a real religious teacher, people tend to be driven by their particular deeply ingrained likes, dislikes and temperaments. These tendencies and inner forces have been moulded by thousands of incalculable factors over their numerous past lives. Therefore devotional seekers would seek out only teachers who emphasise Bhakti Yoga; intellectual individuals would only select teachers who stress the importance of Gnana Yoga, and action-oriented persons would only choose teachers who prefer Karma Yoga to other spiritual paths.

Buddhist seekers would similarly be attracted to teachers who reflect the seekers' own karmic predetermined predispositions. To illustrate this point let us consider two typical groups of persons. A teacher-seeking Buddhist with a socialistic bent will feel drawn to a monk who belongs to a group that is 'socially engaged'. Such monks maintain that social work and community service is as important as, or even more important than, solitary meditation. In the same way, a teacher-seeking Buddhist with a meditative bent will find a natural affinity with forest monks. These forest dwelling renunciants not only shun society with all its attractions and passing excitements, but also regard meditation as the be-all and end-all of their lives.

When selecting their teachers, pupils have a strong bias towards certain types of personalities. Nearly always the selected teacher would have a bias that closely corresponds to that of the pupil and hence the likelihood of the guru's misinterpreting the Dharma.

We are the victims of our prejudices. Every prejudice distorts perception. All the prejudices, inclinations, likes and dislikes that lurk in the mind have a delerious effect on perception. Pure perception will always remain an impossibility unless one has a pure mind. Only a mind that is totally unconditioned and fully free from every blinding influence can see things as they truly are. Therefore whenever a teacher is lacking in purity we can be sure that he will also inevitably be lacking in clarity. How many Buddhist teachers have extricated themselves from their conditioning? How many have cast off their entire 'psychological luggage' in the sense that they have got rid of all their accumulated impurities?

Just because a teacher is very learned, does it necessarily follow that he is also a pure person? There is a crying need for teachers of immense erudition, who are not only well versed in the suttas but are also paragons of virtue. Such teachers are rare gems. Finding even one such teacher will be as difficult as meeting an Arhat down the street.

What are we to do under the circumstances? In view of the virtual absence of immaculate Arhat-like teachers nowadays, do we altogether abandon our religious quest? Do we resign ourselves to our terrible predicament and continue languishing in Samsara, hoping for better luck during the epoch of a future Buddha? Do we redouble our efforts to find the perfect teacher on planet Earth, even when sceptics say that we are searching for an imagined person who does not really exist? The serious Buddhist has to face a dilemma.

There is a glimmer of light in this seemingly hopeless situation. In the same way that Prince Siddhartha, following his utter disillusionment with the reputed religious teachers of his day, retired to the forests and fell back on his own inner resources with all the hidden treasures therein, and eventually attained Enlightenment, can we not also follow suit? If this metamorphosis or Illumination takes place in us also, then our interest in teachers and texts and temples will recede from our troubled minds and soon become matters of mere secondary importance.

31

Moral Conduct and the Greatest Goal

The *Kimsilasutta* is about right conduct and attaining the supreme end.

1. Sariputta : *"By means of what virtue, conduct and actions would a man be sure of attaining the highest?"*

The Master said:

2. *"Let him honour the aged*
And not be envious.
Knowing the proper time
For seeing teachers,
He should listen
Attentively
To their Dharma discourses
And well-expressed words."

3. *"Let him at the proper moment*
Go to the presence
Of his teachers
With humility,
Without being stubborn and headstrong,
And follow what is taught —
The Dharma,
Self-restraint
And celibacy."

4. *"Dwelling in the Dharma,*
Let him take delight
In the Dharma,
Let him not retreat
From the Dharma,
Let him know what is taught
In the Dharma,
Let him not involve himself
In defiling discussions on the Dharma,
Let him be led
By well-expressed truths."

5. *"Having put a stop*
To laughter,
Mumbling,
Lamentation,
Corruption,
Deception,
Hypocrisy,
Greed
And pride,
Impetuosity,
Roughness
And vice,
Let him live
Free from infatuation
With a serene mind."

6. *"The gist of words*
That are well-understood
Are well-expressed.
The comprehension
Of what is well-expressed
Is the essence of meditation.
But when a man is hasty
And careless,
His understanding
Fails to grow."

7. *"Those who are devoted to the Dharma*
Preached by the worthy ones,
They remain unexcelled
In thought,
Word or deed.
They are established
In tranquillity,
Tenderness
And supernatural calm.
They have attained the essence
Of study
And wisdom."

32

Arise ! Sit Up !

The verses in the *Utthanasutta* caution us against becoming slothful or lazy.

1. *"Arise! Sit up!*
   What is the need for you to sleep?
   What sleep is there for the sick,
   Who are suffering
   As though pierced with an arrow?"

2. *"Arise! Sit up!*
   Be steadfast in the quest
   For inner tranquillity!
   Allow not the King of Death,
   Who knows your lazy leanings,
   To fool you
   So that you fall
   Under his influence."

3. *"Drop this craving*
   Because of which gods and men continue
   To remain in the sphere of existence.
   Do not miss the chance!
   Those who miss the opportunity
   End up in hell
   Where they will suffer."

4. *"Idleness (Pamada)*
   Is the dust of defilement.

By means of vigilance (Appamada)
And wisdom
One must pull out one's arrow."

The Pali word *Pamada* can have several meanings such as 'carelessness', 'remissness', 'indifference', 'slothfulness', 'indolence', 'idleness' and 'delay'. All these meanings are subtly interconnected. A person who is lazy or slothful at work, for example, tends to be slow and therefore naturally delays doing his duties. In the present discussion I have confined myself to 'slothfulness', but the reader is requested to explore the applicability of other meanings.

When idleness (*Pamada*) disappears, there is that exalted quality of *Appamatto*, which means 'vigilant', 'careful', 'thoughtful', 'heedful', 'earnest', 'zealous', 'strenuous', 'diligent', 'quick' and 'active'. The Buddha attached great importance to diligence. 'Diligence' was one of the last words he uttered. Just before he passed away the Buddha addressed some of his disciples. His last words were,

Vayadhamma samkhara
Appamadena sampadetha

"All component things are subject to change,
Strive on with diligence."

Although there is no clear-cut division between the mind and the body, for these are inextricably linked, it is safe to say that human laziness is either body-based or mind-based. Although this discussion is mostly concerned with mind-based laziness, it is necessary to touch on body-based laziness.

Because of inferior nutrition, poor people feel very weak and sluggish. They find it difficult to pay attention for a long time because their minds tend to give in to their fatigue.

Those who oversleep experience a certain drowsiness, whereas those who undersleep become nervous and irritable, for they have a persistent tiredness and are rarely wide awake all the time.

Alcohol and hallucinogenic drugs detract from the alertness of the mind, such as it is. Many are the ways of producing 'altered states of consciousness' so that one can temporarily escape from all that is ugly and unpleasant in ourselves. It is more comforting to dwell in a world of make-believe than to face the hard reality of what we actually are, seeing ourselves as we truly are, warts and all. Watching the thought process as it moves from thought to thought, seeing it without distortion, so that we come to terms with, say, our resentments and aversions and insatiable greed, is far more important than having artificially induced ecstatic states.

It is difficult to remain watchful in situations where there is a dearth of oxygen — stuffy rooms, noisy and crowded places with inadequate ventilation, filthy hovels and the like. The body suffers and the mind's sharpness slowly becomes blunted. Because the yogis describe oxygen as 'the food of the brain' they naturally prefer quiet, mountainous and rural surroundings to large towns or cities. Significantly, it was in the open air and near trees that three important events in the Buddha's life happened — his birth, Enlightenment and demise.

Let us consider the question of what we have termed 'mind-based laziness' or mental idleness. We are discussing the quality or fact of being vigilant. Why is the mind non-watchful most of the time and watchful only occasionally, if ever.

A vigilant mind is an unoccupied mind. There is vigilance only during those moments when the mind is free from all attachments. In other words, the mind is vigilant only when it is in a state of silent nothingness. Alertness springs from nothingness. An alert mind is truly meditative. Such an alert or vigilant mind is always awake and not given to spells of slumber. Why or when does the mind lose that vital quality of constant vigilance?

Constant vigilance ceases whenever the mind gets clogged up with anything that fills up its essential emptiness. Without ceaseless vigilance the mind cannot function efficiently, quickly and intelligently. Vigilance ceases whenever the mind is cluttered with beliefs and problems, or when it is stained with anger, jealousy, resentments, aversions, cravings and the like. Stainless innocence is the hallmark of the vigilant mind.

Vigilance is synonymous with being aware. Awareness is the best form of meditation. Our inner impurities dissolve by themselves and disappear when the light of awareness is focussed on them.

Awareness might have a beginning but it has no ending, operating as it does both by day and by night. The following is only an instance of awareness in operation. An angry man comes into my house and starts scolding me. He uses abusive language. Suddenly my mind is poisoned with hate. The presence of the man is hateful to me. But the moment I am acutely aware of the existence of that hate, seeing it fully, without in any way either condemning or justifying it, and also understanding its origin and all its ramifications, that negative state vanishes by itself. I do not have to eliminate hate, for it goes away of its own accord. This is an example of how changes take place effortlessly whenever there is awareness.

Because the mind is burdened with impurities, constant vigilance is difficult. Because of the absence of constant vigilance, the mind is burdened with impurities.

Both these two statements are true. It is a vicious circle. We are in a paradoxical situation indeed.

Our thought processes can be rightly described as endless chains of changing thoughts. Now, between any two thoughts there is usually a brief interval of sacred silence, which is a pure and thought-free state of very short duration. It usually lasts only for a few fleeting seconds.

During these very precious and truly tranquil moments distortionless seeing or pure perception takes place. Any increase in the frequency and intensity of our meditative vigilance brings with it a corresponding increase in the purity of the mind, which in turn means that these tranquil thought-free states of short duration become tranquil thought-free states of long duration.

After the Buddha had provided them with a suitable subject of meditation, two monks went into retreat for the rainy season. Both of them lived in a forest monastery during this period.

The rain retreat (*Vassa*) lasts for three months. During the monsoons, when the stifling weather can be quite wet and humid, it is the practice for monks to reside in just one place and devote themselves even more intensely to their inner purification and meditation. It is a special period. Incidentally, a monk's seniority in the Order (*Sangha*) is determined by the number of rain retreats that he has spent.

Of the two monks who went into retreat, only one monk was serious-minded. He had a strict code of conduct, whereas the other monk behaved in a frivolous manner.

The serious-minded monk would meditate during the first watch of the night (6 p.m. until 10 p.m.), next he would rest during the middle watch or the second watch of the night (10 p.m. until 2 a.m.), and he would meditate again during the last watch of the night (2 a.m. until 6 a.m.). The frivolous monk, in contrast, would warm himself by the fire during the first watch of the night, when he would also enjoy having conversations with young novices. He would idly while away the hours.

The serious-minded monk, who had been ever-mindful, attained the exalted state of Arhathood before long.

The monsoon season came to an end. The two monks visited the Master with the intention of paying homage to him. The Buddha inquired about the time they had spent together in the forest monastery. The frivolous monk complained that the other monk had been whiling away his time, simply lying down and sleeping.

"What about yourself ?" asked the Buddha.

The frivolous monk said that during the first watch of the night he would sit by the fire and warm himself, and that then he would lay awake.

Little did the untruthful monk realise that the Master was able to see through him.

Thereupon the Buddha told the frivolous monk,

"You are like a weak and slow horse,
Whereas my son (the other monk)
Is comparable to a strong and swift-footed horse."

"Attentive among the inattentive,
Awake among those who are asleep,

The wise surpass the foolish
As a swift horse surpasses
An old and worn-out one."

— Dhammapada, 29

"A monk who delights in attentiveness,
Who fears inattentiveness,
Progresses like fire,
Burning his fetters
Both great and small."

— Dhammapada, 31

"A monk who delights in attentiveness,
Who fears inattentiveness,
Cannot slip back
Into a former state,
Being near to Nirvana."

— Dhammapada, 32

33

Some Basic Instructions that Rahula Received

Rahula was the Bodhisattva's only offspring. The 'Bodhisattva' was the Buddha's designation prior to the attainment of Buddhahood. Rahula, the Bodhisattva's only son, was born on the very day his father renounced the world by giving up his household life. The news of his son's birth reached the Bodhisattva when he was enjoying himself near the royal pond. Instead of rejoicing over the happy news, as any ordinary parent would have done, he decided then and there to renounce the world immediately, for he regarded the son's birth as a bond (*Rahula*).

Following his Illumination, the Buddha accepted the invitation of his father King Suddhodana and decided to visit Kapilavatthu. On that occasion Rahula's mother urged her son Rahula to go to the Buddha and ask for his inheritance. This the boy did but the Buddha remained silent. After having his meal the Buddha left the palace. Rahula followed his father and repeated his request. The Buddha thereupon asked Sariputta to ordain the boy.

The Buddha took a great interest in the welfare and development of Rahula with the result that he preached many suttas for his son's benefit. This was something much more than a mere paternal interest for the Buddha was aware that Rahula, even in his past lives, had had the quality of obedience. Rahula, for his part, was keen on receiving guidance from the Buddha and other teachers.

At the tender age of seven years Rahula had the privilege of listening to a special discourse preached to him, which is called the *Ambalatthika-Rahulovada Sutta*, wherein there is an instruction that he should never tell a lie, not even in jest.

In the *Maharahulovada Sutta* the Buddha, among other matters, explains to Rahula the importance of regarding all forms (*Rupa*) as *not* having a soul or any other abiding substance.

When the Master realised that his son was at last ripe and ready for Enlightenment, he preached to him the *Cula-Rahulovada Sutta*. After listening to this discourse, Rahula and thousands of celestial beings (*Devas*), became Arhats.

Rahula predeceased the Buddha.

In the following *Rahulasutta* the Buddha recommended a life of complete renunciation to Rahula.

1. The Master: *"Don't you look down on the wise one*
Because you always live with him?
Do you care to honour him
Who holds high the torchlight for mankind?"

2. Rahula: *"I do not look down on the wise one*
Because I always live with him.
I always honour him
Who holds high the torchlight for mankind."

3. The Master: *"Having given up the objects of the five senses,*
So lovely in appearance
And so pleasing to the mind,
And having from your home
Gone forth with faith,
Be one who puts out suffering."

4. *"Keep the company of virtuous friends,*
Select a secluded and distant dwelling
With little noise,
And eat in moderation."

5. *"Crave not for robes, alms food,*
Medicinal needs and a dwelling place,
Lest you go back to the world again."

6. *"Respect the disciplinary code*
And restrain the five sense-faculties.
Be mindful of the body
And be replete with revulsion."

7. *"Shun that which appears to be pleasant,*
Attractive and is fraught with passion.
Give your undivided attention
To that which is unpleasant."

8. *"Contemplate the signless*
And cast off the tendency to conceit.
Then by fully understanding pride
You will wander around
In a state of calm."

With these stanzas the Exalted One frequently instructed the Venerable Rahula.

In the text the meaning of 'signless' is not very clear. According to Professor Max Muller the term 'signless' (*Animitto*) refers to the 'unconditioned', which is that indescribable state that is 'free from marks or attributes'. It is freedom from the three signs or marks — Lust or Greed (*Raga*), Hatred or Anger (*Dosa*) and Delusion (*Moha*).

"Without wisdom there is no meditation,
Without meditation there is no wisdom.
Whosoever has both wisdom and meditation
Is on the threshold of Nirvana."
— Dhammapada, 372

"Do wake yourself up!
Do examine yourself!
Being self-protected and mindful, O monk,
You will live happily."
— Dhammapada, 379

"You, indeed, are the protector of yourself.
You, indeed, are your own refuge.
Therefore restrain yourself,

As a merchant restrains a fine horse."
— Dhammapada, 380

"The one who even as a young monk
Devotes himself to the teachings of the Buddha,
Lights up the world,
Like the moon in a cloudless sky."
— Dhammapada, 382

34

Did Nigrodhakappa Attain Nirvana ?

In the *Vangisasutta*, which we will be looking at presently, Vangisa approached the Buddha and raised the anxious question as to whether or not his recently deceased teacher, Nigrodhakappa, was successful in attaining Nirvana. Vangisa had unfortunately not been present as his teacher lay dying.

The consideration of some biographical details about these two personalities would not be out of place in this chapter, especially because this information would make the discussion more meaningful.

Nigrodhakappa was the teacher of Vangisa. They lived in the monastery at the Aggalava shrine. Kappa was his name. The prefix Nigrodha was given because he attained Arhatship at the foot of a Nigrodha (banyan) tree. It was his practice to spend much time in his cell. After returning from his alms rounds, he would go into his cell and remain there until the evening or the next day.

The following few paragraphs concerning the life of Vangisa are excerpts from an earlier book of mine titled *Nirvana, the Highest Happiness* (New Delhi : New Age Books) :

> A brahmin called Vangisa from Rajagaha had an extraordinary power. Just by tapping the skull of a corpse he could tell if the dead person had been reborn as a god or a human being. He could also tell whether or not the deceased was in a miserable state of existence. The brahmins cashed in on his power by taking Vangisa to various places. People paid large amounts of money to discover the whereabouts of their deceased relations.

Once Vangisa and the brahmins were in the neighbourhood of the Jetavana monastery where the Buddha was staying. Noticing the crowds that were flocking to the monastery to see the Buddha, the brahmins started persuading people to visit Vangisa instead, and thereby make good use of his services. Then the people exclaimed, "Does Vangisa know anything ? Our Buddha is unsurpassed and he alone is the Enlightened One." The brahmins were in dispute with the people. They argued a lot. Eventually they all decided to go to the monastery to find out if Vangisa or the Buddha knows more. Apparently it was an attempt to ascertain whether or not Vangisa was superior to the Buddha.

The Buddha had knowledge of what was going to happen. Acting presciently, being fully aware of the intentions of the brahmins who were visiting him, the Buddha asked a monk to bring the skull of a person reborn in hell, the skull of a person reborn in the animal world, the skull of a person reborn in the human world, the skull of a person reborn in the celestial world and also the skull of an Arhat. These five skulls were placed in line and Vangisa was required to tell where exactly these dead persons were reborn. It was probably the most difficult challenge in his entire career.

Regarding the first four skulls, Vangisa was able to tell correctly where the deceased persons had been reborn. However, Vangisa was confused and did not know what to say about the Arhat's skull. Little did Vangisa know that Arhats never have to undergo rebirth ; more accurately expressed, Arhats cannot be reborn as they have exhausted their karma. The Arhats have extricated themselves from the cycle of births, deaths and rebirths. They are no longer enmeshed in *samsara*.

The Buddha said, *"Vangisa, you don't know, but I know where the owner of that skull is."* When Vangisa pressed the Buddha to teach him how to tell where that person was reborn, the Buddha asked him first of all to enter the Order.

Vangisa became a *bhikku* and the Buddha advised him to meditate on the 32 parts of the body. He did likewise and before long Vangisa became an Arhat.

It was Nigrodhakappa who ordained Vangisa. Needless to say, the latter reverentially regarded the former as his preceptor.

Vangisa was a poet and he liked to express himself in verse. The Buddha paid him a great compliment when he declared that Vangisa was foremost in ready expression.

While Vangisa was meditating in solitude, the following thought occurred to him: "when my preceptor Nigrodhakappa passed away, had he attained the Nirvanic state of perfect peace or not?" Vangisa was deeply troubled by this matter. In the evening Vangisa visited the Buddha who was residing in the monastery at the Aggalava shrine. Vangisa joined his hands in salutation towards the Master, and then proceeded to pose the above-mentioned question.

1. Vangisa: "We ask the incomparable Teacher,
Who in this world has removed all doubts:
A famous monk of peaceful mind
Has passed away at Aggalava."

2. "O Exalted One,
It is you who called him Nigrodhakappa.
It is you who showed that sage
(*Brahmana*)
The unchangeable state.
He wandered forth, adoring you,
Hoping for release
And expending much energy."

3. "O Sakyan of limitless seeing,
We are also keen to know about that
disciple.
Our ears have a yearning to hear,
O Master beyond compare."

4. "O lord of vast wisdom,
Tell us if he was
In the state of perfect calm
When he died.
O lord of infinite sight,
Speak to us,
As speaks the thousand-eyed Sakka
Among the gods."

5. "All the bonds of the world
That cause delusion,

Along with ignorance
That cause uncertainty,
These dissolve before the 'Perfect One'
Or 'He who has come and gone
As have previous Buddhas' (*Tathagatas*)."

6. "If in a man the defilements do not
disappear
For good,
As the clouds get dispersed in the wind,
The whole world will be
Shrouded in darkness,
And even men of light
Will fail to shine.."

7. "The wise become the enlighteners.
Hence, O hero,
I regard you as such a person.
We have come before you
As you can see clearly
And understand.
Concerning Kappa,
Please do disclose it to this assembly."

8. "O beautiful one,
Like a singing swan
With its neck outstretched,
Quickly use your lovely voice.
All of us will listen to you attentively."

9. "I will make him teach the Dharma,
Who being pure,
Has gone beyond the cycle
Of births and deaths.
Earthlings cannot do what they wish
But Tathagatas can do what they intend."

10. "Perfect will be your explanation of it.

Perfect sage,
It will be accepted.
This final salutation of clasped hands
Is well offered.
As you know it,
Do not mislead us."

11. "Having fully understood the noble
Dharma,
O you of unexcelled strength,
Do not mislead us since you know it.
As a sufferer
Of the scorching summer thirsts for water,
I am filled with longing
To hear your words.
Shower knowledge on us."

12. "For whatever purpose
Kappa led a chaste life.
Was that all in vain?
Did he eventually attain
The state of serenity,
Or was there still remaining
Some substrata of grasping?
Let us hear how he attained Liberation."

13. The Master: *"He dropped the craving
For name-and-form
In the psycho-physical organism.
He totally transcended birth and death,
Thus going across
The Evil One's (Mara's) stream,
Which had lain dormant for a long time,"*
declared the Exalted One, the Teacher of the first five disciples.

14. Vangisa: "Hearing your words,
O Supreme of Seers,

I am satisfied.
My question was not in vain.
The Buddha (Brahmana) did not mislead me."

15. "The actions of the Buddha's disciple
Were in accord with his words.
The strong and stretched out net,
Of deceptive death
Was broken asunder."

16. "On Kappa's seeing
The origin of craving,
O Enlightened One,
Kappa did indeed
Go beyond the sphere of death
That is so difficult to go across."

35

What is the Right Road for a Recluse ?

The *Sammaparibbaganiyasutta* is an excellent code of conduct for monks. It is of great benefit to laypersons also.

1. Questioner: "I ask the Buddha (Muni) of vast wisdom,
Who has gone across to the other shore,
Who has attained serenity and is steadfast:
How does a monk,
Who has given up both home
And sensual pleasures,
Live rightly in the world?"

2. The Master: *"He who has lost faith in omens,*
Meteors, dreams,
The practice of making predictions
By means of signs,
And who cares not about luck —
Lives rightly in the world."

3. *"The monk*
Who has no attachment
To sensual pleasures
Both human and divine,
Who has gone beyond
The cycle of existence
Since he has understood the Dharma —
Lives rightly in the world."

4. *"The monk*
Who is no longer given to slandering,
Who is free from anger and avarice,
And who has neither likes nor dislikes —
Lives rightly in the world."

5. *"He who has dropped*
Both the agreeable and the disagreeable,
Who does not cling to anyone or anything,
Who is absolutely independent,
And who has cast away his chains —
Lives rightly in the world."

6. *"Whenever there is clinging to anything,*
Within it he sees
No permanent substance or essence.
Being rid of the desire and passion
For attachments,
Being independent
And never being led by another —
He lives rightly in the world."

7. *"He who is devoid of hostility*
In word, thought and deed,
Whose comprehension of the Dharma
Is complete,
And who is oriented towards Nirvana —
Lives rightly in the world."

8. *"The monk*
Who does not feel flattered by the thought
'He pays homage to me',
Who is not angry
When abuse is hurled at him,
And who does not get intoxicated with pride
After receiving food from others —
Lives rightly in the world."

9. *"The monk*
Who casts off covetousness

And has no craving
For the life to come (becoming),
Who does not injuriously cut and bind others,
Who is not given to doubting,
And who has dropped the darts of defilement —
Lives rightly in the world."

10. *"Knowing the conduct that becomes a monk,*
He would never cause anyone any harm.
Understanding the Dharma
As it really is —
He lives rightly in the world."

11. *"He in whom no latent traits are lurking,*
The evil roots of which are no longer existing,
Whose cravings have ceased
And who has no longing for any —
Lives rightly in the world."

12. *"With the ending of the cankers (Asavas),*
With the cessation of conceit,
With the transcendence of passion,
There is serenity and steadfastness,
And he is completely calmed (Parinibbuta).
Such a one lives rightly in the world."

The term *Asavas* refers to 'cankers', 'taints', 'corruptions', 'intoxicants' and 'biases'. There is a list of four cankers:

Canker of sense-desire	*Kamasava*
Canker of desiring eternal existence	*Bhavasava*
Canker of wrong views	*Ditthasava*
Canker of ignorance	*Avijjasava*

13. *"Full of faith,*
Well versed in religious literature,
Seeing the path to Nirvana,
Partisanless among the partisans,
Greed and hatred and repugnance

Having fallen away,
Such a one lives rightly in the world."

14. *"The conqueror of the highest purity,*
Remover of the veil of deception,
Master of mental phenomena,
Who has reached the other shore,
Who is without craving,
Who has realised the ending
Of the dispositions,
Such a one lives rightly in the world."

15. *"He who has freed himself*
From the figment of time
As regards the existence of the past
And the existence of the future,
Who has excelled himself
In pure understanding,
And who has released his grip
On all the sense bases,
Such a one lives rightly in the world."

16. *"Knowing the path,*
Understanding the Dharma,
Seeing clearly the falling away
Of the cankers,
Being free from ties,
Such a one lives rightly in the world."

17. Questioner: "Certainly, O Exalted One,
It is truly so that a tamed monk
Who lives in this manner,
Having broken all bonds —
Lives rightly in the world."

****

When the Buddha stated that he would die soon, the news came as a complete surprise to many.

"Four months hence I shall pass away" he said.

It caused considerable consternation among numerous monks. Monks by the thousands started attending to the Master's needs. It is reported that those who had failed to attain 'the Fruit of Conversion' were unable to control their tears. Some went about in small groups saying, "what are we to do?" There was a deep sense of despair because of the realisation that they had, as it were, failed to make hay while the sun was shining.

Now there was an out-of-the-ordinary monk called Dhammarama, which means 'He-Whose-Garden-of-Delight-is-the-Dharma'.

Dhammarama was aloof and distant from his fellow monks.

"Brother, what is the matter with you?" they inquired.

Dhammarama remained silent, but the idea occurred to him, "the Teacher has declared that he will be no more after four months. But I am still enslaved by desire. Therefore while the Master is still with us I will work hard and attain Arhatship".

For that reason he set about thinking carefully and seriously about the Dharma.

The monks reported the matter to the Buddha and complained, "Dhammarama has no affection for you. Since he heard from us about your impending death he has had nothing to do with us."

The Buddha summoned Dhammarama and asked whether they were telling the truth.

"Yes," replied Dhammarama, who then proceeded to explain the reason underlying his behaviour.

"Good, good!" exclaimed the Buddha in approval.

On that occasion the Buddha said,

"Monks, every monk
Must show his affection for me
In the manner of Dhammarama.
They who honour me with garlands,
Perfumes and the like
Fail to honour me.
But they who truly practise
And live the Dharma
Truly honour me."

During the course of his discourse the Buddha uttered the following stanza:

"The monk who lives in the Dharma,
Who regards the Dharma with delight,
Who meditates on the Dharma,
Who well remembers the Dharma,
He does not fall away
From the good doctrine."

— Dhammapada, 364

At the conclusion of the discourse, the monk Dhammarama attained Arhatship.

References

The Book of Protection, translated by Piyadassi. Kandy : Buddhist Publication Society, 1981.

The Buddha and His Teachings by Narada. Colombo : Vajirarama, 1973.

The Buddha's Path of Virtue : A Translation of the Dhammapada by F.L. Woodward. Adyar : Theosophical Publishing House, 1949.

Buddha's Teachings, being the Sutta-Nipata or Discourse Collection ... by Lord Chalmers. Delhi : Motilal Banarsidass, 1997.

Buddhist Dictionary: A Manual of Buddhist Terms and Doctrines by Nyanatiloka, 3rd edition revised by Nyanaponika. Taipei: Corporate Body of the Buddha Educational Foundation, circa 1987.

Buddhist Legends translated from the original Pali text of the Dhammapada Commentary by Eugene Watson Burlingame. Oxford: Pali Text Society, 1995.

Buddhist Saints in India : A Study in Buddhist Values and Orientations by Reginald A.Ray. Oxford: Oxford University Press, 1994.

The Connected Discourses of the Buddha : A New Translation of the Samyutta Nikaya by Bhikku Bodhi. Boston : Wisdom Publications, 2000.

Daily Buddhist Devotions by K. Sri Dhammananda. 2nd edition Kuala Lumpur : Buddhist Missionary Society, 1993.

The Dhammapada by E.W. Adikaram. Colombo : Gunasena, 1999.

The Dhammapada by F. Max Muller. Delhi : Motilal Banarsidass, 1980. (In *Sacred Books of the East,* vol. 10.)

The Dhammapada by K. Sri Dhammananda. Kuala Lumpur : Sasana Abhiwurdhi Wardhana Society, 1992.

The Dhammapada by Narada Thera. 3rd edition, Kuala Lumpur : Buddhist Missionary Society, 1978.

The Dhammapada by S. Radhakrishnan. London : Oxford University Press, 1968.

Dictionary of Pali Proper Names, by G.P. Malalasekera. New Delhi : Munshiram Manoharlal, 1983.

A Dictionary of the Pali Language by Robert Caesar Childers. London : Trubner, 1875.

The Discourse Collection: Selected Texts from the Sutta Nipata... by John D. Ireland. Kandy : Buddhist Publication Society, 1983.

Encyclopaedia of Religion and Ethics, edited by James Hastings. Edinburgh : T & T Clark, 1925-52.

Everyman's Ethics : Four Discourses of the Buddha... translated by Narada. Taipei : Corporate Body of the Buddha Educational Foundation, undated.

The Greatest Man who Ever Lived : The Supreme Buddha by Weragoda Sarada. Singapore : Singapore Buddhist Meditation Centre, 1998.

The Group of Discourses (Sutta-Nipata), vol. 2, by K.R. Norman. Oxford: Pali Text Society, 1995.

A Manual of Buddhism by Narada. Kuala Lumpur : Buddhist Missionary Society, Malaysia, 1995.

The Seeker's Glossary : Buddhism. 2nd edition, New York : Sutra Translation Committee of the US and Canada, 1998.

The Sutta Nipata : A Collection of Discourses. 2nd edition revised, translated from the Pali by V. Fausboll (In *Sacred Books of the East*, vol. 10) Delhi : Motilal Banarsidass, 1980.

Suttanipata : Pali Text with Translation into English... by N. A. Jayawickrama. Kelaniya : University of Kelaniya, Sri Lanka, 2001.

Woven Cadences of Early Buddhists... by E.M. Hare. London: Geoffrey Cumberlege, 1947.

References

Nyanaponika, *Buddhist Dictionary: A Manual of Buddhist Terms and Doctrines*, Taipei: Corporate Body of the Buddha Educational Foundation, 1987.

Nyanatiloka 3rd edition revised, Taipei: Corporate Body of the Buddha Educational Foundation, circa 1987.

The Seeker's Glossary : Buddhism. 2nd edition, New York : Sutra Translation Committee of the US and Canada, 1998

Piyadassi Kandy (transl.) *The Book of Protection*, : Buddhist Publication Society, 1981.

Weragoda Sarada, *The Greatest Man who Ever Lived : The Supreme Buddha*, Singapore : Singapore Buddhist Meditation Centre, 1998.

K. Sri Dhammananda 2nd edition, *Daily Buddhist Devotions*, Kuala Lumpur : Buddhist Missionary Society, 1993.

Narada, *The Buddha and His Teachings*, Colombo : Vajirarama, 1973.

Narada,(translated) *Everyman's Ethics : Four Discourses of the Buddha*, Taipei : Corporate Body of the Buddha Educational Foundation, undated.

Narada, *A Manual of Buddhism*, Kuala Lumpur : Buddhist Missionary Society Malaysia, 1995.

Lord Chalmers, *Buddha's Teachings, being the Sutta-Nipata or Discourse Collection* Delhi : Motilal Banarsidass, 1997.

K.R. Norman, *The Group of Discourses (Sutta-Nipata)*, vol. 2, Oxford: Pali Text Society, 1995.

V. Fausboll, (translated from the pali In *Sacred Books of the East*), *The Sutta Nipata : a Collection of Discourses 2nd* ed. revised, Vol 10 Delhi : Motilal Banarsidass, 1980).

E.M. Hare, *Woven Cadences of Early Buddhists*, London: Geoffrey Cumberlege, 1947.

John D. Ireland, *The Discourse Collection: Selected Texts from the Sutta Nipata* Kandy : Buddhist Publication Society, 1983.

Bhikku Bodhi, *The Connected Discourses of the Buddha : A New Translation of the Samyutta Nikaya*, Boston : Wisdom Publications, 2000.

James Hastings, (ed.) *Encyclopaedia of Religion and Ethics*, Edinburgh : T & T Clark, 1925-52.

Reginald A.Ray, *Buddhist Saints in India : A Study in Buddhist Values and Orientations,* Oxford: Oxford University Press, 1994.

K. Sri Dhammananda, *The Dhammapada*, Kuala Lumpur : Sasana Abhiwurdhi Wardhana Society, 1992.

E.W. Adikaram, *The Dhammapada*, Colombo : Gunasena, 1999.

Narada Thera, (3rd edition) *The Dhammapada*, Kuala Lumpur : Buddhist Missionary Society, 1978.

S. Radhakrishnan, *The Dhammapada*, London : Oxford University Press, 1968.

F. Max Mueller, *The Dhammapada*, Delhi : Motilal Banarsidass, 1980 (In *Sacred Books of the East*, vol.10).

F.L. Woodward, *The Buddha's Path of Virtue : A Translation of the Dhammapada*, Adyar : Theosophical Publishing House, 1949.

N. A. Jayawickrama, *Suttanipata : Pali Text with Translation into English,* Kelaniya : University of Kelaniya, Sri Lanka, 2001.

G.P. Malalasekera, *Dictionary of Pali Proper Names*, New Delhi : Munshiram Manoharlal, 1983.

Robert Caesar Childers, *A Dictionary of the Pali Language*, London : Trubner, 1875.

Eugene Watson Burlingame, *Buddhist Legends translated from the original Pali text of the Dhammapada* Commentary, Oxford: Pali Text Society, 1995.